The Road to Craigellachie
revisited

Hans Offringa

The Road to Craigellachie
revisited

A journey of discovery through the world of Scotch whisky
with an occasional detour to some other interesting places

Conceptual Continuity

Colophon

©2011
Hans Offringa
Conceptual Continuity

Design: Laurien Stam
Layout: Becky Offringa
Photography: Hans Offringa

First published in 2005 as *The Road to Craigellachie*

ISBN 978-90-78668-10-7

www.hansoffringa.com
www.thewhiskycouple.com

To William Ross,
my Scottish faither

Table of Contents

Prologue

The Road to Craigellachie was originally released in the Netherlands in 2004 as *De Weg naar Craigellachie.* At the London Book Fair my then-publisher sold the English language rights to a small one-woman company with the unusual name Lipstick Publishing. The launch was scheduled for the Speyside Festival in May 2005, together with Michael Jackson's magnum opus *WHISKY – The Definitive World Guide.* We had a wonderful time at the happening that took place in the famous Craigellachie Hotel.

Unfortunately soon after that things went downhill with my publisher. She had already ill-advised me about the cover, which understandably evoked a lot of laughter. My image in full Scottish regalia had been taken in a studio in the Netherlands and was super-imposed over a picture I once took on the Isle of Skye (!) of a winding road. A fellow whisky writer had the guts to open it, read it and write a review stating, "It looks like an odd-ball of a book, but I like it." Sales numbers soon dropped. Disaster didn't stop there. Half a year later news reached me that Lipstick had gone out of business and sold its brand name to a dubious magazine publisher. The remaining stock of "The Road" as well as my publisher disappeared without a trace and I never received any royalties. So much for one of my first contributions to the world of English whisky literature.

In the meantime the Dutch version sold well and became a kind of cult book in both the Netherlands and Belgium. Whisky-loving people told each other: you have to read it not only if you want to go to Scotland but also if you have already been there. Well, that's something a writer loves to hear! So I licked my wounds from the Lipstick adventure (they had also published my historical book on the raising of the *Kursk*, which went the same route as "The Road") and went on with my life, basically tasting whiskies, travelling, doing research, presenting, writing and translating.

Approximately three years ago I started to get requests via Facebook, Twitter, our website and email about that "obscure book called The Road to That-Village-with-the-Unpronounceable-Name". People wanted to buy a copy but could not obtain one, except a few offered by online shops asking super-inflated prices (from 115 USD to 148 GBP). I never intended it to become a collectors item, but it had, which I found simultaneously ridiculous and cheering. I answered the emails, telling that I had been cheated and was trying to reacquire the rights. That took a bit of time, but finally I managed and that opened the door to republishing the book. My wife and muse Becky did some fine tuning and we decided to bring the book back to life with a better cover and call it *The Road to Craigellachie-Revisited*. Nothing much has changed in the book itself, apart from correcting some obvious errors. However, we did replace the photographs and add a new epilogue at the end to inform you what happened in due course with some of the characters in the book.

And now we are back on the Road, or should I say with the Road? Anyway, it was a great pleasure to announce the official relaunch in that mythical place, the Craigellachie Hotel in the eponymous village, during the Speyside Festival 2011.

Thank you all, especially my friends in that wonderful village and immediate surroundings, for your support, hospitality, enthusiasm and cordial friendship.

Craigellachie is in my heart, forever.

Hans Offringa, April 2011

The Craigellachie Hotel

Craigellachie
Thursday, 1 May 2003, 2:00 pm

A hamlet with an unpronounceable name. A tiny village in Speyside, the heart of the Scotch whisky industry. A beautiful Victorian hotel with a world-famous whisky bar. A distillery. A famous arched bridge with characteristic stone towers, built by Thomas Telford, one of the great Scottish architects. A bit further, the smallest pub of Scotland. And more than four thousand miles to the west, a village with the same name, in Canada.

I am in the library of the Craigellachie Hotel in one of the most spectacular areas of Scotland, and I am looking through the window. Down below, I see the river Spey, which gave its name to this region. Opposite, to the left, I can see the contours of Easter Elchies House, Home of The Macallan, Rolls Royce among Scotch single malt whiskies. On the antique desk in front of me is my laptop, ready and eagerly awaiting the next batch of letters that I will turn into words and readable sentences.

Fourteen years ago, I visited this picturesque village for the first time. Just passing through. And I stayed in a B&B – the Craigellachie Lodge with no inkling of all the things this country would bring me in the years to come.

Now, in 2003, I am bound to this country and this hotel in many different ways. I have graced it with many a visit, have met a variety of notorious whisky buffs, made friends, and tasted a lot of whisky. I am here this week because of the Speyside Festival and to assist Duncan Elphick, manager of the Craigellachie Hotel, in the vari-

ous festival activities. The Festival's first anniversary is coming up, and it can boast a growing number of visitors, who find their way to 'The Craig' from all corners of the globe this first week in May. For me it's a reunion; I'm meeting old friends.

My thoughts turn to a time way back, to thirty years ago. To the year 1974, the year I first became acquainted with 'uisge beatha'.

Ballantine's
1974

"Have you ever tasted this?"

Tom Douwma held up a long, dark brown bottle. We were in the large attic of his parent's home, still enjoying yesterday's success as two school friends who had just passed their finals.

I took the bottle from him and studied the label. 'By appointment of his Royal Highness Prince Bernhard of the Netherlands' it said. 'Ballantine's Blended Scotch Whisky.'

"No, never!" I put the bottle on the table between us. At 18, my physical condition was outstanding, due to the many sports I played. I did not smoke, or not much anyway, and the only alcohol I used was the occasional beer after a game of football or tennis. My parents had let me taste jenever, wine and cognac, but I did not like them.

"We have reason to celebrate." Tom put two small glasses on the table and filled them. Fascinated, I studied the golden liquid.

"Nice colour."

"Wait till you taste it. Take a small sip and let it roll through your mouth before you swallow it."

I cautiously smelled the stuff. A pleasant, yet sharp scent filled my nostrils. "It smells good."

"Here's to you."

Slightly hesitant, I put the glass to my lips, not being used to hard liquor.

The taste exploded in my mouth, my gullet was on

fire and my stomach was strangely, but pleasantly glowing. This was Good!

I took another sip and gave a thumbs-up. My journey of discovery through the boundless whisky landscape had begun.

Glenfiddich
1974

Neither Tom nor I really knew what we wanted to do after our finals. We would like to see a bit of the world before we started to work or continue our studies. To get money to travel, we accepted a job as salesmen of the Dutch version of *Football International*. Selling subscriptions door-to-door, each one brought in twenty-five Dutch guilders, black money of course. After four months of this we had saved quite a bit and chosen a destination: Great Britain. English was an easy language for us and we could afford the price of the crossing. We bought a second-hand Sunbeam Imp, which looked like a tub but was of English make, which would be convenient if we needed anything repaired along the way. We booked tickets for the ferry and packed. The night before we left, I spent the night at Tom's. Before we went to bed, he rummaged through the contents of his backpack and took out a triangular green bottle. "You're familiar with blended whisky now," he said, "so the time has come for a single malt."

I nodded, not understanding what he meant.

"This is even better, try it."

This bottle had a label of black and gold, with the head and impressive antlers of a stag on it. Under the picture, in white letters, it read Glenfiddich, Special Reserve, single malt. It didn't mean anything to me, but this whisky tasted a whole lot better than Ballantine's. Smoother, with a pleasant hay-like nose.

"Much better indeed," I confirmed.

In 1974, Glenfiddich was one of the few whiskies to be brought onto the market as a single malt outside of Scotland. This was mainly the result of the prophetic powers of the Grant family, the heirs of William and Elizabeth Grant who had founded the company in 1886. Glenfiddich single malt was introduced on the international market around 1965. Today, it is the biggest-selling single malt in the world, and it is available in over two hundred countries.

That night, in Tom's bedroom, I didn't know a thing about the difference between a blend and a malt. I just liked the latter better. And my curiosity was awakened. For the heck of it, Tom gave me a glass of Ballantine's to taste the difference. And I suddenly liked the taste a lot less than before.

The next day, we left the Europoort in Rotterdam to spend six months in the surroundings of Bury St Edmunds and Cambridge. Our British adventures are described in my first novel so I will limit myself here to the whisky side of the story.

We arrived in Bury and found a room over a pub that same day. In the months that followed, I learned to speak English fluently, I learned to drink a respectable series of blended whiskies and I learned to pronounce their names properly. The barkeeper also explained to me the main difference between a blend and a malt. The first was made from a variety of grains, the other from just one: malted barley. In the years that followed I would discover step-by-step that this was far too simple a representation of the process.

The majority of whiskies served in the pub were blended. The pub had one malt, Glenfiddich of course. The second difference was the price. Malt whisky was much more expensive. At the time I did not know that this was because of the way it is produced and the long time it takes to age in the casks. Our travel budget was better suited to drinking the blended version, so that is where I started on my fact-finding mission.

By drinking, I became familiar with the taste and names of various whiskies such as Teacher's, Bell's, Dewar's, 100 Pipers, J&B and Vat 69 (which derives its name from a whisky tasting house where no less than 100 whiskies were tasted from the same number of casks. The group tasting the whisky unanimously decided that number 69 was the best one and a new blend came into being).

After six months, our money had almost run out and we decided to go home. Armed with my newly acquired knowledge I boarded the ferry. I was pleasantly surprised by the discovery in the tax-free shop of a separate section of 'Malts' on one of the shelves. Curious to know about whiskies other than Glenfiddich, I studied the names. They did not mean anything to me and the staff wouldn't let me taste them. I ended up buying two bottles, paid for with my last pennies: Glen Moray, because it came in a beautiful tin and Longmorn because I was taken by the name.

Back in the Netherlands, I immediately called a willing victim to bear witness to the presentation of my extensive knowledge about whisky.

"Rudolf, I'm back and I brought a couple of great malts," I boasted, without even having tasted them.

Glen Moray and Longmorn
1975

At the age of 19, I presented my first nosing and tasting session ever, to an audience of two: Tom Douwma, my first 'teacher' and Rudolf Nieuwenhuisen, dentistry student at the University of Groningen and my best friend since secondary school. At the time, we still called it consumer research. In Rudolf's run-down student room we ceremoniously put three bottles on the table: Teacher's (a smooth blend with a high percentage of malt whisky), Glen Moray and Longmorn. This opened up a new world for Rudolf, since he was only used to drinking wine from his father's well-stocked cellar.

It turned into a cosy evening and night. We all preferred the Longmorn, but this did not stop us from killing the other two bottles. As was my habit, I took notes in a small notebook I always carried with me. Even as a small boy, I took notes of my adventures and put them all in a big box. When I was writing my first – semi-autobiographical – novel, this came in handy. By then I had moved on to using an electronic notepad, my trusted Apple Macintosh, but that's another story.

I cherish my notes on the taste of Longmorn and Glen Moray. They represent my first attempts at describing the aromas and flavours of whisky. There was hardly any literature on the subject available in those days and one had to make do with the rare advertisement that carried some product information. And that information was far from objective.

The morning after our drinking bout I woke up – without a headache. This was certainly different from my first *tour d'horizon* on the blended whisky trail in England. And thus I discovered a third important feature of the malt whisky – purity. In six months time, I had learned three important lessons: malt whisky is made of malted barley only, it is expensive compared to a blend and it does not give you a headache. My frame of reference had been extended to no fewer than three different malts. This surplus of knowledge led my friends to suddenly regard me as a 'whisky expert'.

Although this was all fun, I couldn't make a living with it. Tom and I applied for a variety of jobs because we were virtually out of money when we returned from England. Tom quickly found a job as barkeeper in one of the bars in Zwolle: the Irish Inn. I was torn between continuing my studies and working. I also wanted to do something with what I had learned during the time in England. My mother, with whom I had moved in temporarily, advised me to follow evening classes. This would enable me to work during the day and to find out what I liked best. I decided to attend evening classes in English at an upper secondary vocational college. I found an ad from a publishing and printing company in the newspaper asking for a proofreader for its division of trade magazines. I was hired immediately and was able to pay my tuition fee the following month. It did not take me long to find a room and within three months of my return from England I was fully independent and earned enough to drink a glass of whisky on a regular basis.

I joined Tom at the Irish Inn every weekend and step-by-step I extended the list of whiskies I had tasted and described. My vocabulary was limited: sharp, smooth, sweet, stimulating and I did not distinguish between what I smelled and what I tasted. Nosing whisky is at least as important as tasting if you are to describe whiskies. The nose is much more sensitive than the tongue and the palate. In fact, for each of our taste buds there are over 10,000 receptors in the nose! The olfactory memory of humans is the best-trained one and the last sense to leave us when dementia sets in. You can test your memory by recalling the smell of the attic in your parental home.

In Groningen, Rudolf also started to study malt whiskies and pleasantly surprised me on my twentieth birthday with a bottle of Glenmorangie. He had been taught to drink this by an extremely wealthy university friend whose family had the habit of drinking this great malt from northeast Scotland as if it were water. With Rudolf, I shared this new passion for 'uisge beatha', which is the Gaelic name for whisky. I had learned that from one of the magazines I was responsible for at work: the Dutch *Doctors and Automobiles* magazine, a lifestyle magazine *avant la lettre* for medics. The article I had corrected described a journey through Scotland. Since there is no avoiding whisky in that country, the article paid a great deal of attention to the origin of the drink. This taught me that the Irish were of the opinion that they had discovered the process of distilling whiskey and that the Scots had stolen and commercialised it. It is more likely that the process was adopted from the Chinese or Egyptians and copied in Europe. People in the Far East had been using the distilling process for many centuries to extract scents. By the 11th century, monks in Europe were distilling wine. One of the products was 'aqua vita' or water of life, which is the literal translation of 'uisge beatha' and 'usqebaugh' – the Irish-Gaelic version. In 563, St Columba left Ireland to sail east and landed on the island of Iona, from where Christianity was disseminated throughout Scotland; it's nice to believe this is how distilling came to Scotland, but there's no written proof. In the course of time, the term became 'uisge', later changing into whisky. The Irish usqebaugh became 'whiskey'.

Tom Douwma was more interested in booze in general and he quickly ran out of things to teach me. The brands of whisky offered by the Irish Inn were fairly limited: Jameson, an Irish blend; Glenfiddich and Glen Garioch, two Scotch malts; four blends, including Ballantine's and Johnny Walker Red Label; and a bourbon, Four Roses, which became my introduction to the market of American whiskeys. A year and a half after our return from England, Tom got fired because he drank more than he sold. He married a lady who also liked the bottle and moved to Lelystad in the Dutch polders soon after. I lost touch with him and would not see him again until twenty years later under very sad circumstances.

Rudolf and I dauntlessly continued on the whisky trail and started a tradition of sending each other an as yet untried bottle of whisky every birthday, blended or malt, depending on our financial situation at the time. After five years, my little notebook contained descriptions of 38 whiskies, in no particular order. The time had come to develop a system for classification.

Craigellachie
Thursday, 1 May 2003, 3:30 pm

The barkeeper brings me back to the present with, "Fancy a wee dram, sir?"

I get up and walk with him to the Quaich Bar on the other side of the hallway. The walls are literally adorned with bottles of single malts, neatly organised by alphabet on shelves that have been tailored to fit the shape of the room. Top left, next to the door: Aberfeldy. To the far right, next to the whisky cabinet: Tullibardine. In between are all the big and not-so-big names, some in 20 different versions, varying in age or type of cask. All of them can be tasted by the glass, ranging from two to one hundred and fifty pounds per dram.

It is about four in the afternoon. The sun is shining. It is too early and too warm for an Islay; so I stick to a nice, light yet complex Glenlivet 12. I go to one of the tables and open a ring binder made of green imitation leather entitled 'The Quaich Bar Tasting Notes'. There is one on each table and they are there for guests to write down their impressions and share them with the other guests, across time and space. They contain some real gems. The dates show that there are some enthusiasts who can drink a staggering amount in one day. For me, after six or seven drams it becomes a matter of survival.

"Aye aye sir, six or seven a day is fine, but after that it degenerates into normal drinking", I once wrote, quoting a Scot whose name is still unknown to me.

I am nestled on the sofa when an old acquaintance comes in, Mark Lawson. Not entirely unexpected because we are to organise a whisky nosing and tasting session tonight for the owners of the hotel, a group of Danish investors.

We greet each other heartily and I order Mark's favourite Speysider: Longmorn 15. Before Mark said farewell to his working life, taking early retirement, he was a marketing manager at Seagram's and in that capacity, he organised nosing & tasting sessions across the globe for Glenlivet which was then still owned by the Canadian company. Now he does PR for the Scottish Tourist Board and runs a small publishing house in Elgin that I helped set up a couple of years ago. Much of what I put into practice and have learned about Scotland and the whisky industry, Mark taught me. Over the years, he has played a crucial role in turning me from an enthusiastic amateur into a whisky buff with a deep love for the country and its inhabitants.

The barkeeper brings us a list with available malts - about four hundred of them. It is our agreeable duty to choose seven for the tasting. I browse through the list. The names call to mind memories of times, people, books and articles from Whisky Magazine, The Malt Advocate, *and the* Newsletter of the Scotch Malt Whisky Society.

Inchgower
1983

In the early eighties of the previous century there were hardly any publications about whisky available in the Netherlands and the few articles I read simply fell in my lap because of the work I did. I had moved on from proofreader to production coordinator and I had become responsible for the production of a number of magazines, among which one for golfers. I gave up my studies of English after a few years because I was thoroughly enjoying myself in the graphics industry and wanted to specialise further in publishing. I had also started to write columns in a trade magazine about electronic publishing in 1981.

An article in *Golf* magazine gave me a new piece of essential information that would come in handy when I started to rearrange my notes on tasting. The article extensively discussed the term malt whisky. I had noticed that some labels said 'pure malt' while others said 'single malt' or 'malt'. I learned that a 'single' malt comes from one and the same distillery. 'Pure malt' simply indicates that the bottle contains malt whisky,which does not necessarily mean there are no other types of whisky in the bottle, and the term 'malt' indicates a certain amount of malt and this may be of any age or any distillery. I also learned a new term: 'vatted' malt, which relates to whisky for which a number of single malts have been blended. The article further clarified what grains were used for what type of whisky: malted barley for malt whisky, corn for American whiskey, rye for Canadian whisky and a mixture of grain and malt whisky for most blends. Irish whiskey is partly different from Scotch in that there is usually no peat used in the 'drying of the malted barley'; the second difference is the use of the 'e' in the spelling. The first difference was not entirely clear to me then, but I had noted that 'e' in the spelling. Because of the many Irish who immigrated to the United States at the end of the 19th century, the Americans adopted the spelling. Canada welcomed a large number of Scots as immigrants and thus adopted the Scottish spelling of the word. In other parts of the world, whisky is usually written without the 'e'. In Scotland, in the early days, people also used the 'e'. It can still be seen on some old labels.

The articles I got hold of often dealt with the subject fairly superficially. This was logical in view of the editorial formula. The only other source of information was the library, but I did not find much there. Real books about whisky were few and far between, or had not yet been re-printed, such as the extensive *The Whisky Distilleries of The United Kingdom* from 1887 written by Alfred Barnard, who, at the time, worked for *Harper's Weekly Gazette*, a magazine for the wine and spirits trade.

The Decanter Magazine, published in Great Britain, came out with an appendix about whisky entitled *Harrods Book of Whiskies* around 1978. This publication was also nowhere to be found.

I stopped my search, mainly because I had changed jobs in 1982 and moved to The Hague to start working for a media consultancy firm. At my farewell party at the publishing house in Zwolle, I was given a bottle of Johnny

Walker Black Label, a tip from a computer programmer with whom I had spent the last twelve months working on an electronic publication for the Stock Exchange. It was a nice, uncomplicated blend, which to me tasted much better than its red brother.

In the meantime, my friend Rudolf had finished his studies and established himself as a dentist in Gramsbergen, a one-horse town, near the German border. He had to go to Utrecht every now and again for refresher courses and at one point he made an interesting discovery in a shopping mall: a small store that sold miniature bottles of whisky of various brands and types. After my move, I regularly received a miniature bottle in the mail with a request for comments. This proved a fine way to stay in touch because we lived far away from each other and my new job took up most of my time. The firm had hired me because of my knowledge of the financial market and my experience with electronic media. One of the clients of the firm was an investment company in Amsterdam. The owner, a wealthy, elderly Belgian, regularly came to The Hague on Friday afternoon to have a drink with us. He always brought a bottle of whisky.

Guy Laroche became my second teacher. Once, after I had organised a training session for his employees, some day in 1983, he took me to a whisky bar and adjoining restaurant in the Korte Leidse Dwarsstraat in Amsterdam. The place was called L&B (List & Bedrog, meaning double-crossing in Dutch). Laroche was respectfully welcomed. He was obviously a favourite among guests and he pointed at five single malts: Glen Deveron, Inchgower, Bunnahabhain, Glenlivet and Glenmorangie.

The barkeeper drew two beers for us, got out 10 sherry glasses and put them on the bar. While we were drinking our beer, he poured the whisky in the glasses, two of each kind. I did not see which whisky was poured into which glass. We sat at a table and a tray with the glasses was set before us, each containing a little bit of whisky. Laroche took the first glass and carefully but decidedly let the liquid swirl in the glass. He explained to me that the length of the 'tears' running along the glass was an indication of the alcohol percentage: the longer the tear, the more alcohol. He held the glass up to the light and studied the colour. He then swirled the glass again and held it under his nose. After nosing the whisky at length he took a jug of water and poured a tiny bit into the glass, swirled again and nosed again. He then nodded approvingly and brought the glass to his lips, sipped the whisky and let the whisky flow through his mouth just as Tom Douwma had told me to do in 1974. He then swallowed and encouraged me to do the same. He watched me without speaking as if this were a religious ritual. It was a wonderful, smooth and somewhat sweet whisky. "Glenlivet", said the barkeeper, by way of explanation.

When I tried the second whisky, Laroche told me to keep my mouth open while I nosed. The result was amazing. The whisky revealed a great deal more of its character. Since then, I always keep my mouth open when I nose the whisky in my glass. The small amount of water that is added makes the whisky open up and results in the aromas being more noticeable. At the time I did not have the vocabulary to describe the scent and flavour in detail, but I was able to distinguish the differences among the five malts. After over an hour we had tried them all, compared them and drank them. Laroche wanted to know which one I preferred and I pointed to the fourth glass. "Inchgower" barked the barman. After an extensive dinner, we left the restaurant in high spirits. Under my arm, I carried a carton containing a bottle of Inchgower. A present from Laroche. The carton became the first one of a collection: today hundreds of single malt whisky cartons and boxes adorn the walls of my study.

Craigellachie
Thursday, 1 May 2003, 4:30 pm

How does one compose a balanced assortment for a whisky tasting? The choice depends on a number of factors. Are the people in the audience experienced whisky drinkers with educated palates, are they beginners or is there a mix of the two? Are they interested in a certain type of whisky, such as the single malt, or are they interested in a wide variety, for instance Irish, American, Japanese and Scotch whisky combined? Or do they want a vertical tasting – which entails getting to know one brand of whisky in depth, by comparing the various years?

For readers who have never attended a whisky tasting and would like to try: Dr David Wishart provides an excellent guide in Whisky Classified. *In this book he explains, based on an intricate tasting profile that he developed in cooperation with the Scotch whisky industry, how a tasting assortment can best be composed. The book further describes ninety-odd readily available, single malt whiskies based on the tasting profile.*

Mark and I have organised whisky tastings before for the Danish owners of the hotel - whom we always refer to as The Vikings – and we mean to surprise them. Do we go international, do we go in-depth or do we give them a series of years?

"Why don't we give them a series of bourbons for a change, in a blind tasting?" I suggest to Mark. At a blind tasting you use dark blue glasses that disguise the colour. The bottles that are used are also hidden from view.

Mark likes a practical joke, but stresses that the head of the Vikings, a short, quick-tempered Dane with a fringe of beard, named Sören Gabriel, really likes single malts. "I don't know if it's such a good idea. I'd rather go for a vertical one."

He is right. The Danes will probably appreciate this. We choose Glenfarclas, a Speysider that is sold in many versions. We choose the 10, 12, 15, 21, 25 and 30- year-old versions, and a final one: a cask-strength version, the '105'. Happy with our choice, we leave the bar to change while the barkeeper gets the glasses and bottles ready.

When we climb the splendid, wooden staircase that leads to the rooms on the first floor, Mark says to me, "Bourbon, that's quite another story."

As I turn the doorknob of my room, my thoughts once again turn to the past.

Jack Daniel
1985

In the two years that I lived and worked in The Hague,
I regularly drank whisky with Laroche. We stayed within a certain spectrum, the twelve single malts that L&B
then had on their shelves. My only whisky experiences
outside of the Scotch malt and blended division were
Jameson, a silky smooth Irish blend and Four Roses, a
delicate American bourbon. In the better restaurants I
had to really look hard to find a malt I had not tasted
before. I earned a good salary and could afford to leave
the blends behind. Every now and again I tried a deluxe
blend such as Dimple, named after the three dimples in
the characteristic bottle, or Chivas Regal in the recog-
nisable silver carton box. Deluxe blends usually contain
more malt whisky than a regular blend, and this results
in a smoother taste.

I felt a bit stuck. Also, I did not really enjoy living in
the western part of the country and I decided to quit my
job, move back to Zwolle and work temporarily as a free-
lance copywriter for an advertising agency owned by a
friend. In my spare time, I did the lighting and sound for
the blues band of an old friend from Zwolle. The drummer of the band was a Keith Richards fan and he emu-
lated his hero to a T. Including his drinking habits. The
drummer told me the lead guitar player of the Rolling
Stones always kept a bottle of Jack Daniel's within reach
and he pointed at his base drum. Inside, surrounded by
the soundproofing material, there was a square bottle

with a black label and white letters: Jack Daniel's Sour Mash Whiskey, Lynchburg, Tennessee. He unscrewed the plastic top, took a considerable sip and offered the bottle to me. I first nosed it and inhaled a sweet, perfumed scent that was nothing like the malts and blends I had gotten used to. Then I took a sip and I felt my cheeks contract. The taste was strange to me, but not unpleasant. Just much more raw than I was used to. There was a card attached to the bottle. I asked the drummer if I could have it. He nodded, and I detached it. It was a tiny American reply coupon. If I filled in a name and address and sent the card to the distillery, a miniature bottle would be delivered to the address listed a couple of weeks later. I grabbed a pen and filled in Rudolf Nieuwenhuisen in the NAME section... Three weeks later, Rudolf called to thank me for a 'strange drink'. A day later, a letter arrived with a brochure from Tennessee. This marked the beginning of a period during which I ignored the malts. Between November 1985 and October 1986 I corresponded quite regularly with the Jack Daniel's Distillery and learned about the secrets of American whiskey. One thing I learned is that because this distillery uses charcoal filtering, their whiskey is not a bourbon.

In the middle of the eighties, bourbons were readily available. I got used to names such as Jim Beam, Wild Turkey, Rip van Winkle, George Dickel, Four Roses and Maker's Mark. The correspondence with David Mahanes, President of the Jack Daniel Distillery, proved a mine of information. Originally, American whiskey was made of rye mainly – rye whiskey. Rye is slightly bitter in taste, which is clearly noticeable when you taste this type of whiskey. Rye whiskeys had become rare however, nearly passing into oblivion due to the rise of bourbon, a whiskey, 51-80% of which is made of corn, with the addition of some malted barley and a modest amount of wheat or rye. Jack Daniel's calls itself a 'sour mash' whiskey. This term refers to the fact that the residue of the previous distilling round is used again in the next cycle. Most bourbon distilleries use this production process. I liked Maker's Mark. It is a pleasantly smooth wheated bourbon and the packaging is very appealing. Each bottle is sealed by hand in the distillery, by dipping the neck of the bottle in liquid red wax. Curiously, at Maker's Mark they spell the word whisky without the 'e'.

Balvenie and Glenlivet
1986 & 1989

The owner of a Chinese-Indonesian restaurant in Zwolle unexpectedly took me back to my first love, Scotch single malt whisky. Jan Tjong Tién, known to friends and acquaintances as Buddha because of his girth, managed to turn his father's restaurant into one with eastern specialties. He was one of the first in the Netherlands to do so. Our family had been eating here ever since we moved to Zwolle in 1960. This is where I had my first Chinese eggroll and my first glass of beer. My father, who was born and bred in Indonesia, preferred to have dinner every Friday night at Tién's. So I had known Buddha since my fourth year, and I saw him almost every week.

My return from The Hague also resulted in my return to Tién's, where I ate once a week. Jan Tjong knew his wines well, he was a certified vinologist, but he was also interested in other drinks. One evening, while I was enjoying my meal, he joined me at the table to chat. As always, he advised a special wine to go with my fish.

"Where do you get this information?" I asked him.

"From reading and tasting" answered Buddha with a smile. He walked away from the table and returned with a pile of magazines and a couple of books on wine. "I have started reading about whisky too. After dinner I will pour a nice single malt for you. This one can compete with the best brandies."

He left me and I browsed through the pile of loosely organised magazines. On the back of one there was a page-size ad for Whyte & Mackay, a Scotch blend. I turned the magazine and to my surprise it said in yellow letters on the front: *Harrods Book of Whiskies* and next to it, 'Published by Decanter Magazine'. I opened the magazine with great anticipation. The colophon told me that this was the fifth edition, revised in 1985. It also said that the first edition had been published in 1978. My research of five years ago proved true! And now I was holding the very thing. 'Book' was too grand a word for it though. It was really a kind of magazine consisting of forty-eight pages, partly in full colour, partly black/ white, with three staples holding it together. On pages twenty-four and twenty-five there was an extensive feature about The Balvenie, a single malt that I did not know, at the time presented in a cognac bottle.

"So, you found it." I heard, "Try it."

Jan Tjong had a tray in his hand with a bottle and a tulip-shaped glass, the belly of which was filled with a gold liquid. "These glasses are better than a sherry glass, especially for the nosing."

The whisky had a great nose, slightly sweet and full of flavour. Indeed, the perfect after-dinner malt.

"Take the magazine, I have finished reading it," said Buddha after we finished our whisky.

I paid, thanked him and hurried home to read the magazine from cover to cover. It contained descriptions of no less than one hundred and ten single malts, with tasting notes added. Most names were completely unfamiliar to me, but it also contained some old friends, like Inchgower.

This magazine gave me the professional vocabulary

to enhance my tasting notes. Apart from the malts, there were over forty blends described in it, among which Ballantine's, my first blend, and it included an especially informative article about the making of single malt whisky, replete with some historical facts. After reading the magazine, I gradually turned my back on the Americans, but only after I sent Jack Daniel's one more request for literature about bourbon. On October 17, 1986, I received a reply with a tip about a book that I have not been able to get hold of as yet. It would be the last letter I was to receive from Lynchburg for many years.

I fully concentrated on Scotland, once again. A year later, in 1987, Dorling Kindersley published Michael Jackson's *The World Guide to Whisky*. Jackson was a British journalist who had become famous for his beer atlas. After writing this, he moved on to whisky to drink and write about – not surprising, because the first part of the whisky-making process is quite similar to that of brewing beer. I found the book at the London Book Fair when I visited the DK booth and I bought it before returning to the Netherlands. Together with *Harrod's Book of Whiskies*, *The World Guide to Whisky* formed the start of my – now substantial – whisky library. Jackson's book was a real treat and my first extensive reference work.

Single malt whisky slowly became popular and the better restaurants started carrying brands other than Glenlivet and Glenfiddich. In 1988, United Distillers brought the Classic Malts series on the market and intensified its marketing efforts to sell the series outside of Scotland. The series consisted of six whiskies that were distilled in different parts of Scotland and each of them has a distinct taste. Glenkinchie (Lowlands), Dalwhinnie (Highlands), Cragganmore (Speyside), Oban (Western Highlands), Talisker (Islands – Skye) and Lagavulin (Islay). Travel agencies played into this and soon the first whisky tours were offered. A small number of distilleries in Speyside joined forces and set up a true whisky trail. Originally Glenlivet, Glen Grant, Strathisla, Glenfiddich, Cardhu and Glenfarclas were included in the trail.

Early 1989, I received a letter and a package from Glenlivet. It contained a miniature bottle. From the letter I surmised that this was a gift from my friend Rudolf.

The booklet Glenlivet promised to send never arrived. I called Rudolf to thank him and suggested it was about time we travelled to the country where this whisky was produced and visit the Glenlivet distillery. We did not want to go with a group on a pre-organised trip so I promised to look into it and come up with a plan.

To help potential travellers, DK published a handy, oblong book in 1989, again written by Michael Jackson: *The Malt Whisky Companion*, which contains brief descriptions of most malt distilleries in Scotland. It has short tasting notes for each whisky with a quality score on a scale from 1 -100. The earlier published *World Guide* is a coffee-table book and too large to take along on a trip. I bought the *Companion* and selected the distilleries of the whisky trail, found a map of Scotland and started planning a trip that would take us via Edinburgh, with its Scotch Malt Whisky Heritage Centre, to Speyside. There, Michael's *Companion* was to lead us to the distilleries, with The Glenlivet, one of my favourite Speyside malts, as the trip's grand finale. Michael's book was to become my constant companion on that first Scotland journey Rudolf and I were about to undertake.

Michael Jackson, by the way, was not the first to write a book with tasting notes about whisky. In 1986, Lochar Publishing published a pocket-sized book written by Wallace Milroy, who is regarded as the first professional writer of whisky tasting notes in the world. The title of the book was *Malt Whisky Almanac, A Taster's Guide*. I did not know about this almanac until 1994. It became my bible soon after, but more about that later.

During one of my visits to Buddha's restaurant I told him about our travel plans. He advised me to go in spring because of the nice weather and the least chance of rain. After dinner, he poured a whisky that is often called the Rolls Royce among the single malts: The Macallan. This is a Speysider with a reputation in its own right, which is a result of its ageing predominantly in sherry-casks rather than in re-used bourbon casks. Exquisite in colour, full and rich in flavour, incomparable to anything else. I wrote down on a napkin: "visit Macallan? leave next spring?" put it in my pocket, went home and devoted myself to the itinerary.

It happened on June 16, 1990. After a one hour-and-15-minute flight, KLM put us on Scottish soil, at Edinburgh airport to be exact.

Craigellachie
Thursday, 1 May 2003, 5:30 pm

In my hotel room I undress, enter the bathroom and take a long shower. Refreshed and robed, I turn to the window. The sun is shining and engages the clouds in a wonderful game, the outcome of which can be seen in the ever-changing colours on the hills and the trees on the other side of the Spey.

The strange feeling I experienced when I first came to Scotland and which is now completely familiar to me, returns once again. It is a kind of melancholy, a connection with the land that can only be understood and felt when you have actually been there.

I dry myself off and walk to the bed on which my Highland dress is laid out. A kilt made of the bright green Ross Modern Hunting tartan, a Prince Charlie-jacket with accompanying waistcoat, a dress shirt, bow-tie, sporran (a pouch usually made of leather and fur that is buckled around the waist), knee socks with flashes in the same tartan, a pair of black brogues with very long laces that have to be tied in a certain way and a 'sgian dubh' The latter is a dirk that is put in one of the socks. The name is Gaelic and it means 'dark knife'. Its use stems from the days that the English terrorised Scotland and had forbidden the use of weapons and the wearing of tartans. I use the sgian dubh occasionally to take the seal off a whisky bottle. I bought the entire outfit at McCall's in Elgin after I had been accepted into the Ross clan. The kilt is customised and it takes four to six weeks to be made. They let me take the accessories with me when I bought the outfit. I found out to my cost what it meant to do this because the sgian dubh was in my carry-on bag and was taken out in Aberdeen. The Scottish customs officer appreciated the mistake but I still could not keep it with me. Upon arrival at Schiphol Airport I had to go and collect the knife, which had been packed in a separate box.

I dress and sit on the bed to tie the laces of my shoes: turn them five times at the front, pull them up, a time and a half around the calf, turn twice at the back, and tie a bow on the outside of the leg. Ready for take-off.

Before I go downstairs, I call the Glenfarclas distillery. I have been friends with John Grant, the current owner, for a couple of years now. I tell him we will be tasting 'his whisky' and ask him to join us for a dram later that evening.

"Probably" he says. My thoughts go back to the time I knew next to nothing about Scotland.

Dalwhinnie and Cardhu
1990

When we got off the plane and I had both feet on the ground, a strange sense of melancholy took hold of me. It felt as if something was pulling me, yet it also felt familiar and old, very old. Rudolf involuntarily looked my way, raising one eyebrow. I shook my head and thus shrugged off that strange sensation after which we quietly passed customs, got our suitcases and let a taxi take us to the centre of Edinburgh. I had pre-booked a double room in the Royal British Hotel at Princess Street, for one night. It seemed like a good place to start our quest for the 'Holy Glenlivet'.

At the bar, which was well-stocked with single malt whiskies, we ordered a 12-year-old Macallan.

"What happened at the airport?" Rudolf asked.

I shrugged my shoulders. "It felt as if something was pulling me. Very strange, but not unpleasant. Actually I felt quite comfortable. Like when you are at home with your folks."

Rudolf had to laugh. He is the common sense part of our pair. But it stayed on my mind; it was indeed as if I had come home. Since I could find no explanation at the time, I stored the thought in the back of my mind and got busy with the *Road Atlas of Great Britain*. We plotted a route for the next day to take us to Speyside. The A90/M90 would take us out of town in the direction of Perth. From Perth we would take the A9 to Inverness and would look for a hotel or B&B there. I had not made the connection between Inverness and Loch Ness but when I saw the (in)famous loch on the map and followed its course north, I discovered that it was in fact linked to the city by the River Ness Canal.

"Since we will be in the neighbourhood, we might as well check out the monster," said Rudolf. We left Edinburgh to itself and went to bed early expecting a long drive for the following day. We also expected the roads of Scotland to be heavy going...

The next morning, after a hearty breakfast, we checked in at the car rental company some hundreds of meters from the hotel, around eight. We paid no attention to the beautiful city around us, for we were totally focused on the whisky trail. Rudolf did not feel like driving on the left side of the road and he took the map. I did not care who was driving. Moreover, I had gotten used to driving on the left side when I lived in England. We quickly left the city behind us and crossed the Firth of Forth using the Forth Road Bridge. To our right we saw a magnificent rail bridge, one of Edinburgh's famous landmarks, which we had also spotted from the plane.

As soon as we had left the city behind, the landscape started to change. The first mountains appeared. The M90, a four-lane expressway, led us to Perth in no time and turned into the most important north-south route of the country, the A9, which alternates between being two and four lanes. The road system was much better than we expected. The pulling sensation of the previous day returned, and was intensified by the magnificent landscape surrounding me. Also, I felt that I knew exactly where I was and where I was going. Around noon, we had travelled past Pitlochry and decided to stop at the next pub for lunch: the Atholl Arms Hotel, diagonally opposite Blair Castle. After having chased a bar meal with a couple of pints, we walked to the other side to visit the castle which is owned by the duke of Atholl, the only nobleman in Great Britain allowed to have his own private army. The castle represents a fine collection of white, connected buildings and the interior is extremely rich and well-kept. The family have entertained guests here for over 700 years. It is one of the best-visited castles in Scotland. History has always interested me and I usually feel at home in old buildings where you can almost touch history.

Some hours later, we left, entirely happy, and yet we had not seen a single distillery and we had already spent two days in the Promised Land. The landscape became breathtakingly beautiful. The tarmac meandered through the green hills that now looked like mountains.

We turned into the Drumochter Pass and suddenly, near a crossing, we saw a pagoda-shaped chimney roof ahead, the main characteristic of a malt distillery. After a few curves we saw it in full glory: Dalwhinnie, one of the Classic Malts, but not yet included in the whisky trail. Full of awe we turned into the car park of our 'first distillery' to discover to our disappointment that it was closed. Sunday! We had not thought of that. The only thing we could do was to take a picture. We drove on, slightly disillusioned, and arrived in Inverness late afternoon, finding a nice B&B at Glen Urquhart Road.

Inverness is much smaller than bustling Edinburgh. We took an evening walk along the River Ness and had dinner at a tandoori restaurant. The next morning we drove south over the A82, along the western side of Loch Ness and stopped in a village called Drumnadrochit situated on a part of the loch that sticks out. On a protruding point, a bit further, is the impressive ruin of Urquhart Castle with a view of Loch Ness on three sides. A while later we were standing on the shore of the loch, like many thousands of people before us, staring at the water to catch a glimpse of the monster. When you keep looking you start seeing all kinds of shapes that seem to move through the water. After a quarter of an hour - during which I saw an actual duck swim by - we had had enough, but it still was impressive. The loch has a radiance that even the greatest stoic cannot ignore. The landscape now started to have an effect on Rudolf too. Scotland either gets to you the first day, or it makes you never want to return.

"I can feel it now too," he said, and added, laughing, "yet we still haven't seen a distillery from the inside!" We walked back to the car and took out the map. To get to the River Spey, we first had to go back to Inverness, and then go east using the A96 to get to the A939 at Nairn and go south. Over two hours later we entered Grantown-on-Spey crossing a small stone bridge. Under us was the famous river that had given its name to the Speyside malts. We parked the car and walked down the bank, next to the bridge. By way of a small stone levee we got to the middle of the river and could scoop up and taste the icy-cold and clear water. We turned it into a ceremony. After all, this water was used in many single malts. It deserved a bit of respect.

In Grantown, we saw the first brown signs saying 'whisky trail'. "This is it," I said to myself and steered the car in the direction indicated by the sign, "the first distillery we see we will visit."

The first one was Cragganmore, also one of the Classic Malts, and in 1990 not yet a member of the 'official whisky trail'. We were not allowed to go inside but we did get a miniature bottle. Hiding our disappointment but proud of our trophy, we drove on to the next sign, a few miles on: Tamdhu! And now we were allowed to come in. Unfortunately here too, we were disappointed. A window! Standing behind the glass, we did get an impression of the still, a washback and a spirit safe. But it looked more like a shop window than a working distillery. Our third day in Scotland was nearing its end and we still had not been on a true guided tour of a distillery. We were starting to give up hope and were looking for a B&B or hotel that suited us. And then, suddenly, we got lucky: after about fifteen minutes we saw the sign that saved us, 'Cardhu, part of the whisky trail'. It was almost four in the afternoon and the final tour was about to begin. We hurried to the entrance and were warmly welcomed. On June 18, 1990, at 4:15 pm, I saw, smelled and felt a pot-still for the first time, or rather its warmth. A wonderful row of red-copper stills. A sight to be remembered and a smell that would never leave the nostrils. Whenever I am near a distillery the sight and smell come to mind immediately. We could not hear or understand the guide, due to the noise and his relentless accent. But we didn't care. This was what we had come to Scotland for. After the tour, we were given a glass of Cardhu to taste, a 'wee dram' and if we wanted we could have another one or two. Nowadays, distilleries charge for the tour and the tasting, but in 1990, you could visit many distilleries at no cost and they poured whisky freely and enthusiastically. Also, there were no elaborate visitor's centres, as there are now. Whisky was drunk where it was produced, in the distillery itself. It had not become a mass tourism event yet.

Surprised and warmed by the hospitality we had met, the free tour and ditto whisky, we got into the car and drove on, quietly and at peace with ourselves, northeastward bound. Twilight was upon us when we saw the contours of a tiny castle on a hill straight ahead of us. At the bottom of the hill, we saw a sign that led us up the hill to a B&B. The owner, a blonde, attractive lady of about forty, introduced herself as Veronica. She did indeed have vacancies. Tired but happy we booked a room with two beds, took a shower and entered a deep sleep. The sleep of the contented. I had no idea where we were. I would not know until seven years later where I put my head to rest that night.

Craigellachie
Thursday, 1 May 2003, 6:30 pm

Downstairs in the Quaich Bar everything is ready for the tasting. Ten sets of seven glasses. Each glass holding two centilitres of whisky. Jugs of Highland Spring Still Water on each table for those who prefer a little water in their malt. The '105' definitely needs it, because it has been bottled at cask-strength (60%).

It turns out to be a solid selection. While Mark Lawson inspects the glasses, I get Michael Jackson's Malt Whisky Companion *(4th edition) out and study his tasting notes, which follow:*

Glass 1: Glenfarclas 10-year-old. Colour: Full gold. Nose: Big, with some sherry sweetness and nuttiness, but also smokiness at the back of the nose. Body: Characteristically firm. Palate: Crisp and dry at first, with the flavour filling out as it develops. Finish: Sweet and long.

Glass 2: The 12-year-old. Colour: Bronze. Nose: Drier, with a quick, big attack. Body: Firm, slightly oily. Palate: Plenty of flavour, with notes of peat smoke. Finish: Long, with oaky notes, even at this relatively young age.

Glass 3: The 15-year-old, favourite of Ishbel, John Grant's wife. Colour: Amber. Nose: Plenty of sherry, oak, maltiness, and a hint of smokiness – all the elements of a lovely, mixed bouquet. Body: Firm, rounded. Palate: Assertive, again with all the elements beautifully melded. Finish: Long and smooth.

Glass 4: The 21-year-old. Colour: Amber. Nose: More sherry. Butter. Sultana-like fruitiness. Sweet lemon juice on a pancake. Greater smokiness, as well as a dash of oak. All slowly emerges as distinct notes. Body: Big, firm. Palate: Immense flavour development. Raisiny, spicy, gingery. Finish: Remarkably long, with lots of sherry, becoming sweetish and perfumy.

Glass 5: The 25-year-old. More of everything. Perhaps a touch woody for purists, but a remorselessly serious after-dinner malt for others. Colour: Dark amber. Nose: Pungent, sappy. Body: Big, with some dryness of texture. Palate: The flavours are so tightly interlocked at first that the whisky appears reluctant to give up its secrets. Very slow, insistent flavour development. All the components gradually emerge, but in a drier mood. Finish: Long, oaky, sappy. Extra points out of respect for idiosyncratic age.

Glass 6: The 30-year-old. Colour: Refractive, bright amber. Nose: Oaky, slightly woody. Body: Very firm. Palate: Nutty and oaky. Finish: Oaky, sappy, peaty.

Glass 7: The '105', 8 to 10 years old. A very youthful version for such a big malt, but it wins points for firm-muscled individuality. Colour: Full gold to bronze. Nose: Robust; butterscotch and raisins. Body: Full, heavy. Palate: Very sweet, rich nectar, with some honeyish dryness. Finish: Long, and warmed by the high proof. Rounded.

This will give the Vikings something to get their teeth into, or rather their nose and taste buds. Mark nods approvingly at the barkeeper. I check my own tasting notes in Wallace Milroy's almanac. Glenfarclas was not my first choice when I first came to Scotland and I did not even go to the distillery then. I had ample opportunity to rectify that mistake in the years since then. The advantage is that by that time my taste had developed further, so

I could assess this great malt at its true value. As I am browsing through my notes, my eye falls on The Macallan and I remember the days when I had never even heard of such a thing as a vertical tasting.

The River Spey between Craigellachie and Aberlour.

The Macallan
1990

The next morning, while we were eating in the breakfast room overlooking the hill on the other side of the Spey, Veronica came in and joined us at our table. "Across the river is The Macallan, you should go there, laddies. Do you want me to phone them? You need an appointment."

I looked at Rudolf and nodded. This was one whisky for which we could certainly postpone our journey to Glenlivet. One still cannot visit The Macallan unannounced. They prefer to do tours for small groups of no more than ten people, by appointment only. This benefits people's attention as well as the tour. Veronica called them and found out that we were welcome but not until the end of the afternoon. We didn't mind, because we were now in the heart of Speyside and there is a distillery at almost every corner. We let go of our plan to follow the whisky trail, thanked Veronica and drove to Dufftown on spec. Dufftown is a village five miles down the road that has no less than seven distilleries. Or as the Scots proudly say, "Rome was built on seven hills, but Dufftown's built on seven stills."

The first distillery we came across was Glenfiddich, my very first malt. We couldn't resist this one! We turned into the car park, got out of the car and went to the visitor's centre. Because of the fact that Glenfiddich had been active in foreign markets for over 25 years, it drew a great many visitors as early as 1990. The tour was a very professional one. We were first shown a fifteen-minute video that showed all facets of the whisky-making process. A pleasant voice-over explained the process step-by-step, with interludes of wonderful Scottish music. I sat back in my chair, enjoyed myself tremendously and learned that:

To make single malt whisky only three ingredients are necessary: barley, water and yeast. The process of turning those three components into whisky is much more complex and usually is subdivided into various steps, known as malting, drying, milling, mashing, fermentation, distillation, maturation and bottling.

Before it can be used, the barley has to be malted. For two to three days the barley is steeped in large stainless steel vessels containing water. The grain becomes soft and sticky and starts to germinate. Small sprouts grow from the kernels and the starch in the barley grain is converted into maltose (a kind of sugar). Once spread out on the malting floor, the barley is turned regularly to prevent overheating. A handful of distilleries still turn the germinating malt manually by using a wooden spade (shiel) or a motorised device resembling a small lawn mower. Because of its labour-intensive character this traditional process is largely mechanised and centralised. Germination takes about a week during which time the "green malt" becomes saturated with natural sugars, out of which alcohol will be distilled later in the process. Germination is stopped by means of drying the barley. That happens in a kiln, using hot air. When peat is applied as fuel for the fire in the kiln, the eventual whisky will carry a distinctive smoky flavour. Nowadays most distilleries buy their malted barley from large commercial maltings that produce their malt on precise specifications. A distiller can exactly specify the peat level resulting from drying and thus secure the consistency of his whisky's taste. One can purchase stocks of malted barley with varying peat levels. This gives the distiller the possibility to produce different expressions from the same stills, ranging from a non-peated to a heavily peated whisky.

In the next stage the malt is cleaned through a large sieve and transported to a mill that grinds it into a coarse kind of flour called grist. The grist is then mixed with hot water in a huge vessel, the mash tun. The maltose in the grist dissolves in the water and the remaining sweet liquid, called "wort", is drained out of the mash tun. After cooling, the wort is ready for fermentation. The residue in the mash tun, "draff", is used for cattle fodder.

The wort is then pumped into a giant vessel called a "washback". Yeast is added and the liquid starts to foam and froth aggressively. During fermentation the sugars are converted into carbon dioxide and alcohol. This starts a reaction with the acids from the malt, which creates esters and aldehydes. The aromas we associate with flowers and fruit come from a combination of many different esters. More prosaically described, fermentation is nothing other than changing the chemical structure of a liquid by using microorganisms. Fermentation is sometimes referred to as "yeasting". The resulting liquid is called "wash" and resembles a heavy beer, containing approximately 7-9% alcohol by volume.

The wash is pumped to a stillhouse where the liquid will be distilled twice in large copper pot stills. The first round takes place in the wash still; alcohol, esters, aldehydes and acids are separated from the yeast, other impurities and the remaining water. As soon as the fermented liquid reaches a temperature of 87 degrees Celsius, the alcohols in the wash evaporate and ascend through the neck of the still. The alcohol fumes then condense in the form of a raw, oily liquid called "low wines", containing approximately 17-21% alcohol. The low wines are pumped to the spirit still, also known as the "low wines" still, to be redistilled. This second still is usually smaller in size than the wash still. During the second round of distillation the stillman has to catch the middle cut or "heart of the run". For this purpose he uses a spirit safe that was introduced by the British Tax office in 1823 to prevent illegal tapping-off. With the safe the stillman can assess the quality and density of the spirit and decide when he takes the cut. In some distilleries this process is computer controlled.

The first part of the distillate is called "foreshots". They contain impurities and are collected separately to be redistilled in the next round. When the liquid reaches the desired quality and alcohol percentage the stillman switches the tap to the spirit receiver. It takes a lot of skill and craftsmanship, since at this point during the process the quality of the eventual whisky is determined. At the end of the second distillation the temperature inside the stills increases. Several oily elements, the so-called "feints" evaporate. They may influence the flavour of the whisky in a negative way and are collected together with the foreshots to be redistilled with the next batch of low wines from the wash still.

The middle cut, selected by the stillman, is now a colourless liquid containing 60-70% alcohol. It is collected in a spirit receiver, a huge vessel made of wood or stainless steel. From here the liquid is transferred into oak casks, after which the maturation process starts. The spirit has to stay in the casks for a minimum of three years before it can legally be called whisky. Most malt whiskies mature 10-12 years and often longer in purpose-built warehouses. The type of cask, the size, the maturation time and the climatological circumstances all influence the flavour and aromas of the mature whisky. In Scotland distillers primarily use casks that previously contained bourbon or sherry. The bourbon casks are imported from the United States. The sherry casks come from Spain.

During the maturation period the master distiller regularly draws samples from various casks to test the development of the whisky. At a given moment in time he decides that the whisky can be bottled. Before being filled into a bottle, the whisky is usually chill filtered and diluted with demineralised water down to 40-43% ABV. Some distilleries bottle part of their whisky unfiltered and/or undiluted. Those whiskies are called "cask strength, non-chill-filtered".

The percentage can vary from 50 to 70% ABV. It is advisable to dilute such whiskies with water before savouring them.

When the film ended, a guide came to collect us. She first took us to the Mash House, then to the Tun Room and next to The Stillhouse, which contains a line of stills. Compared to Cardhu, the Glenfiddich Stillhouse seemed as large as a soccer field. It was clear that whisky is produced on a very large scale here. We then went to the filling store and the warehouse. Flabbergasted, I stared at the immense number of casks and I asked the guide if they had taken out insurance for all this. That was not possible, she said. In case of a fire, a distillery would simply cease to exist. This is why most distilleries have part of their whisky mature elsewhere, as a kind of backup.

Glenfiddich is one of the few distilleries to bottle a portion of its whisky on the spot. Most malts are transported to Glasgow to be bottled. Here, on this location, we could see the final phase of the process on the grounds of the distillery. The people here are proud of the fact that their malt is "chateau bottled".

The final part of the tour took place in the visitor's centre, where we were treated to a glass of single malt. The centre included a small shop that sold souvenirs and special editions of Glenfiddich, including a bottle in the shape of a golf ball. I bought one to give to the editor of the golf magazine that I had worked for a decade ago and in which I had read my first article ever about the making of malt whisky.

During the tour, we had asked the guide many questions and she had seen me take down the answers in a booklet. When the other guests had left, she asked me why I did this. After my explanation, she smiled and asked if we wanted to see something special. We nodded and she took us outside to check out sister distillery The Balvenie, which is on the same grounds, but not usually accessible to visitors. At The Balvenie, the malt was indeed turned by hand, which is exceptional in the industry. We were allowed to walk on the malting floor and look inside the kiln where the peat fire was burning.

I had a wonderful time and thought of a great little test for Buddha: on my return, I would check to see if he knew that Balvenie and Glenfiddich were sisters.

After the extra tour, we accompanied the guide back to the visitor's centre where we were offered a dram of Balvenie. I asked how it was possible that two distilleries that are located within a stone's throw could produce whiskies so different in taste. This led to a lecture about still sizes, fermentation cycles, the maturation of whisky and the use of various types of casks. Balvenie matures in ex-sherry casks while Glenfiddich matures in former bourbon casks.

Three hours later, after having profusely thanked our guide, we left the grounds of the Grant family, enriched with a great deal of knowledge. The guide asked us where we were going next.

"The Macallan," we replied with one voice.

"That's where my brother has been working for more than twenty five years," she said and told us a remarkable anecdote. Everyone who works at Macallan was given a bottle a month to take home. Her brother didn't drink,

The Macallan has "curiously small stills".

so his house was crammed with full bottles. I don't know if the story is true, but her name is engraved upon my memory: Isobel Gormsley.

We were shown great hospitality at Macallan. The distillery is much smaller than Glenfiddich and boasts the fact that it is the first one to mainly use oloroso sherry-casks for the maturation of whisky instead of the frequently used bourbon-casks. It gives their whisky the colour of full amber and a rich, caramel-like aroma. I feasted my eyes on everything there, and with the knowledge we had newly obtained at Glenfiddich, I recognised the various phases in the process. At Macallan they were especially aware of the quality and the need to guarantee it. In the warehouses, there were casks of many different years, which enabled the staff to compare them constantly and keep the consistency of the taste at the desired level. We were allowed to nose the content of a cask from 1954, which was extra special for Rudolf, since he was born that year. We were not allowed a dram however, none whatsoever. Instead of a dram, we were given a miniature bottle in a small cylinder when we left. This started us on a collection of miniatures. Over the course of the years, Rudolf was to build up a substantial collection until he discovered that one of his houseguests drank nearly all of them. We decided to kill the others together. I now limit myself to miniature bottles of the distilleries I have visited.

Filled with new experiences we returned that night to Veronica's for our supper. Before turning in, we took a walk through the village the name of which I still did not know at the time.

We had three days left in Speyside, two of which we spent alternately visiting various distilleries that were part of the whisky trail: Glen Grant, Strathisla, Glen Moray, Longmorn (of course), and Linkwood (where we weren't allowed in and where we were chased away when I took a picture of the pagoda), and historic buildings such as the ruins of the cathedral of Elgin, which in ages past, had been set on fire by The Wolf of Badenoch, a locally famous tyrant and robber baron, because of a fight he had with the prelate. Those were the days.

We had reserved the third day for Glenlivet, the main goal of our journey. The River Livet is a tributary of the Spey and the water in it is extremely clear and clean. Close to the distillery, under a beautiful, ancient, arched bridge made of stone, we walked into the stream and tasted the water just as we had done four days earlier at the Spey. After this, we took a tour through the buildings, a strange combination of old and new. Glenlivet is also produced on a very large scale. The founder, John Smith, was a colourful and controversial figure. He was one of the first in the region to leave illegal distilling behind by gaining a license from the English government in 1824. His neighbours did not appreciate this and legend has it that he was threatened with death several times and that is why he always carried two loaded pistols. They can still be found today in the first-rate visitor's centre, in a locked glass case. When we left, we both bought a yellow tray with the Glenlivet logo printed on it in addition to a miniature bottle. I still use the tray for tastings at home. The quality of the tray is at least as good as the whisky of that name.

Back in Edinburgh, we booked a night in a hotel that was more modest than The Royal British and situated in a less fashionable part of town. In the afternoon, we visited the Whisky Museum on the Royal Mile to conclude our trip. Sitting in a motorised whisky cask, we were taken past three ages of whisky history represented in neatly produced life-size dioramas.

I did not sleep well that night; I woke up several times. The next morning, a taxi took us to the airport. As we took off, I did not feel that I was going home; on the contrary, it felt as if I was *leaving* home and very reluctantly so. My senses told me I had been in Scotland before, more often and much longer. My mind could not accept it yet.

Craigellachie
Thursday, 1 May 2003, 7:15 pm

*One by one, the Vikings enter, ten in total, with Sören
Gabriel leading the group. They drink a couple of pints
to get them started. These gents are thirsty after having spent the day outside, on the estate owned by Innes
McPherson, a wealthy, extremely amiable gentleman
farmer who makes his estate available to people who
want to try their hand at trout fishing, quad biking, off-
road driving, clay-pigeon shooting or archery. During
the hunting season, experienced hunters are allowed to
shoot game. In the past few years, the Danes saved the
hotel from certain bankruptcy by investing a great deal
of money and by physically assisting in the thorough
renovation of the place. They regard 'The Craig' as their
home away from home, and literally take possession of
the bar. Duncan Elphick, the hotel manager, subtly moves
the other guests to the drawing room, the games room,
the smaller bar downstairs or the library.*

*For the next hour and a half, the Quaich Bar is our
territory. We exchange civilities with Sören and his wife
Birthe, who has joined him on this trip because of the
Speyside Festival, which officially starts tomorrow. Gabriel is a tough but successful businessman, who thoroughly
enjoys the ownership of the hotel and his financially independent status. A few years ago, we engaged in energetic
discussions about the way in which the hotel's name could
be put on the map of the world. At the time, the hotel had
already been largely renovated but the image of decline*

still stuck. Duncan Elphick, with whom I have developed several ideas to make the hotel better known, took less than five years to change the image, which has resulted in The Craig winning various prizes and today being a world-famous phenomenon with whisky lovers from Japan to the United States.

Gabriel did not like all our plans, but he did adopt a few, among which the founding of the 'Friends of the Craigellachie Malt Whisky Club', with members from all over the world. The club's members have certain privileges, and 'own' a tiny part of the hotel in the shape of shelf space. This is a space in the Quaich Bar on a shelf in a cabinet that is locked. Members can keep their own bottle of whisky there. Next to the cabinet, attached to the wall, is a plaque that lists the members' names and cities of origin. As a thank you for the idea, Duncan Elphick gave me space on the shelf, and since then I have always kept a bottle of single malt on the shelf, behind the rack. Whenever one of my friends or acquaintances visits The Craig, I send an e-mail to the reception staff asking them to serve him or her a dram from my bottle upon arrival. The manager makes sure the bottle is never empty.

To be honest, not all of our plans matured well. The introduction of a whisky label encyclopaedia that was to strengthen the hotel's name turned out to be a fiasco. And Gabriel had warned me in advance. He did not want to invest in it. Mark Lawson and I did and in the end this adventure cost us some tens of thousands of pounds. So much for idealism.

The library of the hotel still has a copy, for reference purposes. It may well be one of the few that are left of the

The sign at the entrance to The Craigellachie Hotel.

more than one hundred we sold before we were forced to abandon the project. Gabriel's reaction when he heard about the calamity was brief and to the point: "This is a hotel, not a fucking publishing company," after which he offered me a 21-year-old Springbank to drown my sorrows. We've been through a lot together, Sören, his people and I.

"How long is it again that you've been coming here?" he asks while I am handed a pint.

"Scotland or The Craig?" I answer.

"Both."

"The Craig since 1997, but Scotland since 1990."

"What happened in-between?"

"I'll tell you after the tasting, Sören."

His question opens wide the sluices of my memories, once again.

Suntory
1994

Our trip to Scotland had deeply impressed both Rudolf and I and we promised ourselves we would go again the next year and turn it into a tradition. I used the many photos I had taken to make two copies of a trip report. I gave one copy to my friend for his birthday. As is the case with many plans, this one fell through and we did not go to Scotland the year after. Rudolf was too busy with his dental surgery. I was busy being a media consultant and copywriter.

We still regularly sent each other bottles of whisky and now that we were living much closer to each other, we found regular occasions to taste new finds together. We concentrated on the Scotch single malts. Many Scots feel that the use of 'Scotch' before 'single' is a pleonasm; this is not entirely justified, because there are also some fine single malts from Japan, Australia and New-Zealand.

Over three years passed without my being able to leave the country. My pile of notes grew, as did my desire to return to Scotland. Early 1994, the opportunity suddenly arose. One of my clients in those days was a training institute for vocational education in Friesland. In its development plan, the institute had set aside activities and budgets to integrate new media into the curriculum and to exchange experiences with the use of new media on an international scale. For a number of years, the Friesland College had been in contact with Aberdeen College, a college that provided similar education to people in Aberdeen and its surroundings. They asked me to research the possibility of jointly developing multi-media teaching materials. This could be funded by means of a European subsidy if we could find a third country to participate in the project. We chose the Henningsdorfer Bildungsverein in former East Germany, located in the eastern part of Berlin. This was right up my alley.

Nine months out of that year, I commuted between Leeuwarden, Berlin and Aberdeen. We organised our project meetings in Scotland as much as possible. Each time I had to go to Aberdeen, I planned my work on the Friday and Monday, which gave me the weekend off to rent a car and get to know the country.

I took some great trips and photos, expanded my knowledge of the Grampian Mountains and Deeside, and in the process I got so used to driving on the left side that I occasionally ended up on the wrong side of the road back in the Netherlands. I visited many a distillery, but stayed in the area around Aberdeenshire and the northeast side of the Speyside. Names such as Glendronach, Edradour, Glenrothes and Aberlour were added to my list.

Ever since I had spent a brief vacation on the Channel Isles, in the summer of that same year, I owned a very handy little book that I bought from the Guernsey Press on Smith Street on Guernsey. *Wallace Milroy's Malt Whisky Almanac – A Taster's Guide – fully updated 4th edition* it said on the cover. Inside there were 112 brief tasting notes describing the same number of single malts. Below Milroy's notes was a bit of white space that I used to write down my own impressions. From that time on, this book has been my faithful companion, my little bible, and many of my whisky friends have written comments in it after a dram or tasting.

The book accompanied me on every trip in that special year of 1994, a year that took me to Scotland at least ten times. I started to really feel at home there. The contacts with Aberdeen College were interesting, informative and cordial. Contacts with the Henningsdorfer Bildungsverein were not as easy. The people I worked with had spent the larger part of their life behind the Iron Curtain and they had only recently gained access to the joys of western society. Their way of thinking and working however was still very East German. They did not drink whisky. They did drink vodka, however, which led one of the trainers to say, after having finished half a bottle, "This is the only good thing the Russians left us."

My research steadily progressed and at the end of that year I managed to submit a thorough report that described a number of real opportunities for coopera-tion. I left for Brussels, joined by two teachers from the Friesland College, to present the plan to a representative of the committee that was to assess our proposal. As a result of a major traffic jam between Antwerp and Brus-sels we arrived long after five, and too late to visit the city. We had no choice but to find a hotel and have a look around the next day. This proved a blessing in disguise, because the hotel had an excellent Japanese restaurant, and this is where I had my first taste ever of Suntory, a great single malt from the country of the rising sun. Japan has a rich whisky culture. The Japanese are very fond of Scotch single malts, which makes their imitating the style understandable. Today, Suntory is one of the best-known brands in Japan and a perfect alternative for drinkers who want to try something other than Scotch malt.

The Japanese art of copying does go a little far sometimes. A well-known story among whisky buffs serves as an illustration. Once upon a time, a Japanese businessman was so fascinated by malt whisky that he decided to buy the Scotch distillery that distilled his favourite malt. He tore down the distillery brick by brick, transported the whole thing to Japan and re-constructed it there, a perfect copy of the original one.

To produce a good whisky, one needs to let it mature in the cask. The Japanese businessman needed a decade of patience before he could taste the first distillation. He had carefully picked a location that was very similar to the original spot in Scotland. The big day of tasting his own whisky for the first time drew near...

He was greatly disappointed when the taste of the whisky proved very different from his favourite in Scotland, which had now ceased to exist. He decided on the spot to tear down the distillery, transport it back to Scotland and rebuild it again there. Ten years later, he, over twenty years older now, could once again enjoy his favourite whisky.

The story has never been officially confirmed, but it does show how great the influence of location and microclimate on the maturation of whisky is. The Japanese now own a number of Scottish distilleries, but that's another story.

The next day, after a constructive talk with the committee's representative, we left Brussels and drove back to the Netherlands in high spirits. We were ready to submit the application for the subsidy. If it was granted, I could commute between Scotland and the Netherlands for at least another year, and that was of crucial importance to my development as a whisky expert, or so I thought.

Reality turned out to be different. The Germans withdrew before the project was completed and we had no choice but to kill the project proposal. The Scots did not blame us and asked me to keep in touch, which I promised to do. I have never regretted this, because, indirectly, it resulted in my discovery of the Craigellachie Hotel.

Craigellachie

Thursday, 1 May 2003, from 8:00 pm onwards

The Vikings are preparing to sit down to start the tasting session. Some of them have had one too many already. Mark and I silently wonder if our exquisite collection will be lost on them.

"Let the games begin," says Mark and he takes the first glass, followed by all present in the bar. Mark's way of telling people about whisky is unparalleled. Not only in the things he says about the drink, but about everything else too. With the right amount of humour, mixed with a serious tone, he expertly leads us from one nosing and tasting sensation to another. Halfway through the tasting I take over and guide the group through the last three Glenfarclases. After a little over an hour and fifteen minutes, the twelve of us stumble downstairs, to the Ben Aigan room where dinner will be served.

I sit next to Sören Gabriel and start telling him my story. Meanwhile, we are treated to an excellent dinner, consisting of a starter of Scottish salmon prepared in three different ways, an entrée of scallops with saffron rice and fresh carrots, cooked al dente, and a desert of Scottish cheeses with a fine Glenmorangie Portwood Finish to flow with the meal. In-between the dishes, I cover more than fourteen years and we reminisce about previous festivals, chance meetings, other whisky aficionados and our joint preference for particular single malts, like Lagavulin.

It is around midnight when we go to bed, tired, slightly drunk, but very happy. This is a great start to the Spey-

73

side Festival but we have another two days of work – or fun rather – ahead of us. As I lay down, I start thinking of the islands, with their unique,sometimes heavily peated whiskies.

Talisker and Tobermory
1995

The Henningsdorf-Aberdeen-Leeuwarden project was off and with it, my near future regarding Scotland. I did not like this at all. I had really counted on being in Scotland again in 1995. A solution needed to be found, so I grabbed the phone and called Rudolf.

"Next year it will be five years since we went to Scotland. It's about time we went again."

After a brief consultation with his wife, he said, "May would be fine, around Ascension Day, I can close the surgery for a week then. So far I have no appointments, so start planning."

That did not fall on deaf ears. I got out the map of Scotland that, by now, looked much the worse for wear. I had spent the past year getting to know the area north of Edinburgh and west of Aberdeen quite thoroughly and it seemed a good idea to choose a different area for our second trip to Scotland. Moreover, Rudolf and I had visited Speyside in 1990. My eye fell on the islands off the west coast, the Hebrides. I roughly measured distances and calculated that we could visit three to four islands and part of the west coast in one week. This time, our starting point would be Glasgow, which would mean a second Scottish airport on our roll of honour.

Preparing a trip is almost as much fun as undertaking it. I checked my whisky books and wrote down: Talisker, Tobermory and Lagavulin, or in other words: the Isles of Skye, Mull and Islay. The latter whisky, an explicitly smoky malt that smells of seaweed, salt, carbolic, lysol and campfire, would be our final destination, as Glenlivet had been five years earlier. This would give us a clear goal. As usual, Rudolf approved of my plans immediately.

On Friday 19 May 1995, we landed at Renfrew, west of Glasgow, and pointed our rental car north in the direction of Skye. Halfway, we stopped in Fort William, to have a look at the Ben Nevis distillery, named after the highest mountain in Great Britain. This mountain dominates its surroundings and proves a challenge to many hill walkers and climbers. Some years later, Rudolf, who took up the habit of returning to Scotland every year, would conquer Ben Nevis on his own. We watched the Legend of the Dew of Ben Nevis, an amusing film, which taught us about Long John, a local giant from the 19th century, who was held responsible for founding the distillery. His name lives on in a popular blended whisky.

After lunch in the adjacent restaurant, we continued on our way north following the A82, and turned at Invergarry onto the A87, which we took in westerly direction. This magnificent, curvy road offering breathtaking views led us to Kyle of Lochalsh. Along the way, we passed Eilean Donan, the most photographed castle in Scotland and part of the set of *Highlander*, the television series. On the Kyle, we took the car ferry to Skye, because in 1995, they were still building the Skye Bridge. Towards evening, we arrived in the village of Broadford and slept in the Dunollie Hotel, but not before we had tasted a dram of Talisker in the hotel bar.

The next day, we toured the island and discovered

why it is regarded as the most beautiful of the Hebrides. To reach the far north of the island, we had to stay on the east side. The Cuillin Hills, a ragged mountain ridge that runs across the entire island from east to west, does not allow for a straight crossing. The Cuillins, loved and feared by hill walkers and climbers, looked quite friendly from a distance, but as we came closer, we could see how rough and wild they actually were.

After a while we arrived in the harbour of Portree, which is surrounded by bright colourful cottages and is a favourite of sailors due to its secluded position in the Sound of Rasaay. The A855 led us to the far north, to the desolate ruins of Duntulm Castle. Skye has seen turbulent times and until 1960, many people still lived in shabby farmer's cottages. The population of Skye suffered tremendously from the so-called Highland Clearances in the 19th century. Small farmers (crofters) were forced by landowners to leave the island and they emigrated *en masse* to Canada, Australia and the USA. As tenants, they had no right to the fields and sheep replaced them, because sheep brought in more money than agriculture. Between 1840 and 1883, over 7,000 islanders left, usually involuntarily. The remaining part of the original population moved to the coastal areas and tried to stay alive by fishing. The Skye Heritage Centre keeps the memory of these days very much alive.

The entire island is permeated by history and Rudolf and I enjoyed it tremendously. In the early afternoon, we arrived in Carbost, home of Talisker, the only distillery on the misty island, located in a sheltered protrusion of Loch Harport. We enjoyed our lunch of freshly caught oysters, sprinkled with a single malt and we fully agreed with Alexander Smith who had written a century earlier, "Jaded and nervous after eleven months of labour or disappointment a man will find in Skye the medicine of silence and repose."

We spent the rest of the day touring the island, silently enjoying its natural beauty. In the evening, we reached the south side called Sleat, which reminded me of Friesland. This narrow strip of coast is called the garden of Skye. In a pub on the water, we got acquainted with the hospitality and cosiness that marks life on the west coast of Scotland. While we were having a pint at the bar, we watched a group of natives who were enjoying their dinner in a corner of the pub. After the tables had been cleared, they got out their instruments one by one and started tuning their violin, guitar and mandolin. An accordionist and vocalist joined the group that during the next few hours gave a wonderful concert of traditional Gaelic music. Everyone joined in when they sang the Skye Boat Song. We did too, even though we did not understand a word, but that didn't matter. We were adopted by the community without ado. Skye has a strong oral culture and whenever the group took a break, someone would tell anecdotes about living on the island. One of the storytellers invited me to relate the story of where we were from and offered us a glass of Drambuie.

"Do you know where that comes from?" he asked.

We shook our heads, in a trance from the music and the atmosphere, after which we were told the famous story of Flora MacDonald who had risked her life to keep Bonnie Prince Charlie from the hands of the English. The

Scottish pretender to the throne thanked her by giving her a secret recipe, the only thing of value he had left after the massacre of his army at Culloden. This had happened in 1746, but the man sitting across from us told the story with a passion as if it happened a week ago. When we left the pub in the dead of night, we felt we had made friends for life.

The next morning, after an early breakfast, we drove to Ardvasar to see the gardens of Armadale Castle, after which we took the car ferry to Mallaig. We wanted to drive all day to reach the Isle of Mull that same evening. The coastal road south was another sight for sore eyes and we needed no spoken words to accompany us on that stretch. Until I checked the petrol gauge, which was close to zero. I had miscalculated the distance and we had been using the petrol in the reserve tank for some time. We learned that petrol stations are few and far between in this part of Scotland. The engine stopped running in the village of Glenuig, right in front of an inn of the same name, which, according to the sign, had been built in the 17th century. We went inside and discovered that the sign told no lies. The barkeeper gave us a friendly nod and asked what we wanted this Sunday morning. I explained that we had run out of petrol and could not continue on our journey.

"Not many petrol stations here within walking distance. Besides, they are closed on Sunday," he chuckled and prolonged the suspense before he continued with "No problem, I will help you. Let's go outside."

We meekly followed him to the water. He took a jerry can out of a small motorboat and took about ten litres

Not many petrol stations here...

of petrol from the outboard motor. "Here ye go," he laughed and poured the petrol into our tank. I wanted to pay him but he wouldn't let me. Gaelic hospitality epitomised. After a cup of coffee and a few sandwiches at the inn, and after having profusely thanked the owner once more, we took off.

By way of the only passable road on the Ardnamurchan peninsula, we arrived at Kilchoan at the end of the afternoon, and wanted to take the car ferry to Mull. The adventure with the petrol from the outboard motor had seriously screwed up our schedule however. The last ferry of the day had already left and we were forced to spend the night on Ardnamurchan. Rudolf pointed at a sign that read, 'Sonachan Hotel, the most westerly hotel on the British mainland.' This seemed like a good place and we drove a few miles in westerly direction to arrive at a splendidly secluded, 'very quietly situated' little hotel. It was booked full, holding a group of unworldly botanists. Fortunately, there was a caravan behind the building that we could sleep in for a modest sum. We ate in the hotel, which had a bar remarkably well-stocked with single malts. I tried a Glenfarclas 105, cask-strength, 60%. "Quite an experience!" I wrote in my bible. The same was true for the night in the caravan. It seemed as if every beetle and bug had found a hiding place from the botanists. I did not sleep at all due to their noise and the idea that the bugs would be crawling all over me all night. Rudolf was not bothered much, turned on his side, fell asleep and snored all night. When I went to pay the hotelkeeper, the following morning, less than refreshed, I discovered the hotel did not accept credit cards.

"Not in this part of the world dear," the owner smiled. I explained to her that I had ten pounds of cash left which did not go far enough to cover the bill. Also, I needed the cash to pay for the car ferry.

"Here's the bill, see the account number? As soon as you have arrived in Tobermory, go to the bank in the harbour and make a deposit. Have a nice day."

And that was it. I have travelled far and wide in my time, but I have never come across anything like it, not before then and not since. Rudolf was also totally baffled. With an odd, but pleasant feeling of being appreciated and trusted, we drove the stretch back to the Kilchoan Ferry Terminal. This is a big name for a small stone building, which serves as the landing site for a small ferry that could only hold two cars on its deck. We floated on the quiet waters of the Sound of Mull to Tobermory, in a dense fog. Just before we entered the picturesque harbour, the mist lifted somewhat and we could see the gaily-coloured row of houses along the quay.

The first thing we did after driving off the ferry was to visit the bank and settle our debt of honour. We left the car and walked to the far end of the harbour, where the island's only distillery is located. It is one of the oldest in Scotland and has had a turbulent past. It has often changed hands and has been mothballed a couple of times for a longer period. The result is that there are several years of whisky missing. Originally, the single malt that is distilled here was heavily peated, but today, Tobermory is unpeated. A peated version is still produced, under the name of Ledaig. After the visit to the distillery, we drove south to get the ferry to Oban on the mainland.

It was not until years later, when I was in the west of Scotland for a photo shoot, that I discovered how beautiful the Isle of Mull is. Rudolf and I remember this island for its trust and hospitality.

Having arrived in Oban, we did not have time to visit the local distillery, except for taking a picture. I had booked passage on the ferry to Islay from home and it turned out that the harbour we had to leave from was a lot further to the south. It is one of very few times that I have driven through part of Scotland at great speed. The grand landscape flew by and our haste did not match the pace of life in this part of the world. Fifteen minutes before the ferry left, we arrived at Kennacraig harbour. They let us on. I drove onto the ferry's ramp, slightly tired and parked the car below deck. We got out of the car and went to the lounge, prepared for a three-and-a-half hour boat ride.

Craigellachie
Friday, 2 May 2003, 9:00 am

Today is going to be a busy day. First, there's break-fast with the French journalist Martine Nouet, referred to in her native country as 'la reine d'alambique', who is a terrific cook. She has written an excellent book about food and whisky, Les Routes du Malt. *She used to alternate be-tween Paris and the Isle of Islay, but now resides perma-nently on Islay. She contributes to* Whisky Magazine *and is editor in chief of the French edition. When I arrive, she is already at the table. I visit the richly stocked breakfast buffet, get a piece of toast and some orange juice and join her.*

"Ca va, Hans?" she asks teasingly, knowing that I suf-fered a heavy drinking bout with the Vikings last night.

I nod and ask the waiter to bring me haggis with scrambled eggs, my favourite breakfast. We study the fes-tival programme and concentrate on the exclusive dinner that is to be held in the Avon Room tonight, and which is to be hosted by another celebrity from whisky land, Michael Jackson. It will be a seven-course dinner. For eve-ry course a different single malt will be used, as part of the dish. Instead of wine, whisky will be served to accom-pany the dishes. I did this once before, in 2000, together with Wallace Milroy. The only way to live through this is to water down your whisky until you almost drown it. A tip from Wallace, but a bit hard on a malt. Never mind, it's part of the game. Martine goes through the courses with me and shows me which malts Michael has selected.

Next, we study the seating arrangement. My role will stay limited to hosting one of the four tables. I will concentrate on keeping the conversation going. Michael, Martine and Duncan Elphick will take care of the other three tables. The guests are from all over the world and not every one of them speaks English fluently. I get a Japanese couple, four Germans, two Dutchmen and two Danes, while Martine will take care of a largely French table. Duncan and Michael are given a group of Americans, British and The Rest of the World.

"On commence avec les huitres au Talisker," Martine sighs. "Moi-même, je prefere Lagavulin, mais l'autre aussi est une belle combinaitiou."

I nod and am looking forward to the evening. Until then, I will keep busy, because between eleven am and two pm I have to be in the library to meet Charlie MacLean and to assist him in selecting special bottles for an auction that is to be held in Edinburgh soon. I promised Wallace Milroy to keep him company from three until six, after which he will go to another hotel to host a dinner.

"Tu aimes les Islays, n'est ce pas ? Quand viens-tu a ma maison à Islay?" asks Martine, after which she gets up to leave the breakfast room She has invited me before and I really want to take her up on her kind offer, but as yet I haven't found the time. I get up too and ask the waiter to bring me coffee in the library. I haven't been to Islay, the island with the seven distilleries, since 1995. All kinds of names suddenly spring to mind: Bowmore, Caol Ila, Bunnahabhain...Lagavulin.

Lagavulin
1995

In the lounge, Rudolf and I got out our books. It was fairly quiet on the ferry. I looked around and saw that most people were wearing warm clothes, backpacks and hiking boots. Islay and the adjacent Isle of Jura are favourite spots of experienced hikers. We were also wearing hiking boots, because we had learned five years ago that these were the most comfortable whenever we ventured off the road for a walk. I went back to my book.

Fifteen minutes later, someone accidentally hit my outstretched leg. I looked up and saw the cheerful face of a lady, who was carrying a tray holding three glasses of whisky and a jug of water. "Excuse me, I didn't mean to hurt you," she said, cheerily.

I nodded kindly and wanted to continue reading, but her next question stopped me.

"Are you hill walkers, too?"

"No, just for comfort," I explained.

"We're planning to climb a few hills on Jura," she went on, clearly not wanting to let me read on as yet.

"We're on a whisky trip," I replied. "It seems you enjoy the drink as well" and I pointed to the full tray.

"Do you want to join us for a dram?" Rudolf was now also involved in the conversation. We looked at each other and concurred. The lady put the tray down and stuck out her hand. "Enchanted, my name is Anet McIntosh. Meet my friends over there, Gretha and Ulla. In fact, Gretha is my sister."

We closed our books, stood up and walked over to the table Anet had indicated, and met the other two ladies. All three of them were middle-aged, and they were obviously enjoying life.

"Can I get you a drink, lads?" Anet asked. We both ordered a Laphroaig, Lagavulin's neighbour, which is produced by one of the distilleries we were hoping to visit in the days to come. Not much later, she returned from the bar and we engaged in an animated conversation. Ulla told us that she went hill walking every Monday with six ladies in the area around her house in Perthshire. Every now and again, she went to a more distant area for a couple of days, as she was doing this time, to walk in a less familiar area.

They were surprised about our knowledge of whisky and Scotland and grew more and more enthusiastic. We offered each other drinks in turn. I limited myself somewhat because I still had to find a hotel on the island. When I told Anet that, she asked if we felt like having dinner with them in the Ballygrant Inn, an address recommended by a friend of hers. It was also a hotel and they were bound to have some rooms left. She and her lady friends had booked rooms in another hotel, two miles further inland and they wanted to check in before having dinner. They planned to go to Jura the next day. When the ferry arrived, they took a taxi to their hotel and we drove to the village of Ballygrant and found the Inn of the same name. There was one double room left with two separate beds. After freshening up, we went to the bar to wait for the ladies. Fifteen minutes later, they arrived, attractively dressed, entering one by one. It turned into a very pleasant night with lots of whisky, mainly from Islay. Anet and Gretha taught us the fundamentals of highland dancing and we played a game of darts with Ulla. At two in the morning, the barkeeper finally asked us if he could go home. I ordered a taxi for our new friends and they bade us farewell by kissing us on the cheeks firmly. Ulla gave me her business card and said,

"I run a B&B in Perthshire. Whenever you are near, please visit us. Goodbye."

Time had flown and we discussed the amazing level of energy of these ladies. I put the business card in my back pocket without really looking at it.

We dedicated the next day to distillery visits and managed to visit Bunnahabhain, Caol Ila, Bowmore and Laphroaig, as well as Ardbeg and Lagavulin, before we returned to the mainland. We left Bruichladdich for what it was, mainly because it was closed. All the other distilleries warmly welcomed us. In Bowmore the cooling-water is used to heat an indoor swimming pool to which all villagers have free access. In the Caol Ila stillhouse, we saw the Paps of Jura and I imagined I saw three minuscule figures climbing the hillside. Bunnahabhain lay hidden in a bay on the north side of the Sound of Islay. We reached the distillery by means of a curvy, sometimes hardly passable, meandering road. The staff inhabited the tiny houses that are part of the complex. There used to be a small school as well. In the early days, the ingredients were imported and the whisky was exported by a small boat that nearly outsized the even smaller harbour.

At Laphroaig, we were told that a tour was out of the question. To compensate, they gave us each a miniature

Lagavulin, one of my all-time favourites.

bottle to take home. Ardbeg was closed too, but we were allowed to look around. The highlight of the day was Lagavulin, my favourite malt. The sight of the white warehouses along the coast became forever engraved in my mind's eye. Opposite the distillery, facing the water is a bell hanging all by its lonely self in the ruins of Dunyvaig Castle. Whenever there's a storm at sea, and I think of Islay, I can hear its deep, baleful sound.

Rudolf and I did not suffer from storms during the crossing to the mainland that we reached at the end of the afternoon by landing in Kennacraig. The A83 took us to the southernmost point of the journey: Campbeltown, the smallest whisky region of Scotland.

This region was once blessed with over 30 distilleries. Decline set in at the end of the 19th century however, and today, there are only two distilleries still in operation: Springbank and Glen Scotia. Springbank was our goal; it is a traditional distillery with a special history.

During our visit, we learned that Springbank gained its first licence in 1828, but rumour has it that a man called Archibald Mitchell had been illegally distilling whisky there before then. It is the oldest independent distillery in Scotland and it is still in the hands of the original family. At Springbank, the entire process is handled in the distillery, from malting up to and including bottling; a rarity in the industry.

After this abundance of whisky history, the Royal Hotel in the harbour of Campbeltown was a good place to be. In the bar, we met a jolly lady who answered to the name of Betty and who turned out to be a travelling saleswoman in boilers as well as a great fan of Springbank. To us, this was the perfect end to our journey. The next day, we drove back to Glasgow to catch a plane to the Netherlands. We decided that our next trip would not be as long in the making as this one. When we arrived at Schiphol airport, Rudolf's wife gave me the Dutch translation of Michael Jackson's *World of Whiskies*, a welcome addition to my growing whisky library.

Craigellachie
Friday, 2 May 2003, 11:00 am

"Good morning Hans, may I introduce you to Charles MacLean?" I am taken back to the present by the voice of Duncan Elphick, who has honoured my request to meet the famous whisky writer in a very special way.

"Delighted to meet you," says the man who is commonly referred to as The Gentleman.

Shortly after, we are engaged in an animated conversation and Duncan leaves us to it, but not until after he has put the sign 'private meeting in progress' on the door. Charles enlightens me about the plan. In a few months time, Phillips in Edinburgh will organise a special whisky auction. The auctioneer is still looking for a number of rare bottlings and the Craigellachie Hotel has sent out a mailing as part of the Speyside Festival asking people for special editions of single malts from the region.

It is not unusual for distilleries to bring special editions onto the market to celebrate a certain event or to have limited editions of a different packaging or a certain year. Over the past few years, the interest in collecting these has grown into a mania. People sometimes pay up to 10,000 pounds and more for a bottle. Charles does not expect to receive any of those bottles but he does think that in-demand or rare bottles will be found in the cellars of people who have long lived in this region.

At a quarter past eleven, the first visitor enters slightly timidly, holding two plastic supermarket bags. He hesitantly puts them in front of Charles and respectfully sits down on a chair near the open fire. The Gentleman takes the bottles out of the bags, holds them up, turns them around, checks the seal, lists the special features, which I enter into my laptop, and gives a price indication. Not every bottle is worth being auctioned. Bell's standard porcelain decanter, shaped like a bell of course, is so common that you might as well drink the contents, or so says Charlie.

After we have written down the name and address of the man, and he has been given a receipt, he quietly leaves the room.

In the hours following, there is a coming and going of exotic people and bottles. Charles is characteristically calm and he treats everyone with respect. Around two o'clock, it's enough and we close the door of the library. We have a very interesting yield. In addition to some 25 more or less popular collector's items, there are eight very special bottles, including a bottle of Glenflagler that is in perfect condition. The whisky itself is not so special, but the fact that it has only been produced for twenty years makes it a valuable and highly popular collector's item.

"Thanks Hans, please mail me the data," says Charles and he leaves the library. I check the clock and see that I have another 30 minutes before Wallace Milroy arrives. Filled with new knowledge about the collectors' world, I go to my room, connect my laptop to the phone line and send the document. Personally, I feel whisky is to be drunk rather than collected, maybe with the exception of the miniatures that I have bought at distilleries on my travels with my best friend.

Royal Lochnagar and Edradour
1996

After Rudolf and I had returned to the Netherlands, I could not find any peace. Scotland was pulling me more and more, and there were no direct plans for another visit. My plans to commute between Scotland and the Netherlands for work had been thwarted by a couple of stubborn Germans. Back in the Netherlands, I was busy developing a new publishing concept that did not leave me much time to spend on whisky or Scotland. Apart from a few nosing and tasting sessions in the Netherlands and ...yes, Germany – where, through a Dutch friend who worked in Cuxhaven, I had gotten an assignment to introduce customers of his liquor business to the ins and outs of whisky – nothing much happened in the area I still regarded as my hobby at the time. The only thing was that my fame as a whisky expert slowly grew, albeit among a small circle. After an article in a German paper about a smokers' and whisky night, which had me down as 'the expert', more and more requests for tastings arrived from my neighbours in the east. I regularly went to Germany, but it was in a direction opposite to where I really wanted to go.

Halfway through 1996, however, I received a phone call from Friesland College. One of the departments involved in vocational education wanted to start working with Aberdeen College on a student exchange programme. They planned to monitor progress from a distance by means of videoconferences. They asked me to supervise the project because I knew both parties well and, in view of my profession as a media consultant, they assumed I was keeping abreast of developments in the world of new media. This was the opportunity I had been waiting for. I looked up the phone numbers of my Scottish friends and arranged for a meeting. Three weeks later I flew to Aberdeen accompanied by the director of the engineering department and his right hand. Rae Angus the principal and his financial director Roddy Scott warmly welcomed us. We defined a plan of approach and then got cracking.

The second half of 1996 was marked by distance learning. Once again, I flew to Scotland each month and took every chance to travel and visit distilleries in my spare time. There are not many distilleries in the direct environment of Aberdeen: it is a region where they mainly grow barley. That is why it is often called the grain barn of the whisky industry. This part of Scotland has more hours of sun than the Netherlands and it is a pleasant place to be. Aberdeen is not very large but there is a lot going on. This is mainly due to the offshore industry. Next to the cosy, small airport is a separate heliport for the transport of people and material to and from the oil platforms in the North Sea. I explored Aberdeen with Roddy Scott and discovered its beautiful, old part that is concentrated around the university, one of the oldest in Great Britain. When the sun shines on Aberdeen, the city sparkles. I had often noticed this from the plane just before touchdown. When I asked Roddy about it, he explained that it was caused by a certain crystal in the bricks they use to build houses. That's why Aberdonians call their home Silver City. I got to know various pubs in the harbour, which without exception had a good collection of single malts. I used the alphabetical index at the back of my copy of Wallace Milroy's almanac to tick off the names of the malts I had tried and decided I had to try them all at least once. Roddy Scott (such an appropriate last name!) was great company and he told me many interesting stories about the history of his country. He and his wife had an interesting hobby: they bred Shetland ponies. I learned a great deal from Roddy and became more and more interested in the history of Scotland. At Waterstone's on High Street, I bought a superb book entitled: *History of Scotland* and I finished it in one go. The book helped me understand why the relationship between Scotland and England was as difficult as it was. The people in the two countries had made one another suffer often in the past, although the Scottish clans themselves had never been averse to betraying each other to their hereditary enemy if push came to shove. Years later when watching the film *Braveheart* I recognised a great deal in the film, thanks to Roddy and the history books.

Scotland became much more to me than whisky and landscape alone. I started to make friends there and whenever I flew back to the Netherlands it would feel as if I was leaving home rather than going home. On some trips, the teachers of Friesland College would accompany me to Scotland and two of them wanted to see more of the country (and the whisky). I planned a number of project meetings on Friday and Monday, which gave us the entire weekend for sightseeing. By then it was early 1997, and I had never been to Scotland in the winter.

We left at the end of February and arrived in Aberdeen, which was covered in snow. On Saturday morning we drove to the Highlands. Roddy Scott had advised us to take the A93 and follow the River Dee.

"Turn left in Ballater and you'll end up at Loch Muick. Beautiful spot to do some walking. After that, continue on the A93 and you'll pass Balmoral Castle."

This seemed like a good plan. It was cold out, but the sun was shining brightly and it made the snow extra white and sparkling. After an hour-and-a-half's drive we arrived at the loch. It just sat there quietly, completely surrounded by virgin snow. We parked the car, put on our hiking boots and walked towards the water. We chose the east side. We walked steadily for two hours. In some spots, the snow was a meter high and our legs sometimes disappeared completely, and we would crawl out and up on an icy path, slippery as glass, to where the snow was only thirty centimetres high. It wasn't a simple walk and it was colder than we had expected. I suggested we sit on a fallen-down tree and conjured up a flask filled with uisge beatha. After we had warmed and treated ourselves to a large drink of Glendronach, we continued. The sky got darker and the clouds hid the sun. It became really cold and we weren't even halfway. Then it started to snow. We took shelter behind some bushes and waited for the worst to be over, after which we slogged on through the fresh snow. There was no path to be found, and we sometimes sank a meter and a half into the snow. This wasn't your ordinary hill walking; it was turning into a survival trek. I got acquainted with the changeable nature of the Scottish weather the

97

hard way. The Scots have a saying that you can have four seasons in one day.

Over five and a half hours later we stumbled out of the valley on the other side of the loch with two thirds of a mile to go before we reached the car. Suddenly, there was a stag standing right in front of me, less than five meters away. My companions moved behind and around me and called out that there was an entire herd of deer in the valley below. I moved very carefully, knowing that this was the herd's guard and I was in no mood to meet his antlers. Exhausted, we arrived at the car and at that very moment the sun came through. After we had caught our breath, I drove back to the A93 and headed for Balmoral. Just before we reached the castle, I saw a sign that said 'Royal Lochnagar' and resolutely turned the car left. A few minutes later we arrived at an old, slightly declined distillery. A man on the grounds indicated that we could come in. Before we knew it, we were inside holding a wee dram in our hands and warming ourselves at the stills.

This distillery was given the designation 'Royal' in 1848 after the manager John Begg had sent a letter to invite the queen to a tasting. Some time later, Victoria and Albert arrived at Lochnagar unannounced and granted the distillery one of the speediest royal designations in the history of Great Britain. Royal Lochnagar has been a favourite whisky of the Royal Family and the staff at Balmoral Castle for over 150 years now.

We were on historic ground and enjoyed the tour through the traditional distillery, which was not really suited to receive visitors. It was the first-ever whisky distillery my companions visited and I decided to show them a completely different one the next day.

After an extensive tour, we got back into the car and continued on our way. It was long after six by then. Balmoral was already closed to visitors and it was time to find a hotel. We stopped in Braemar and spent the night in the Invercauld Arms, a great looking old-fashioned country hotel with stone towers. None of us had any trouble falling asleep after our exhausting walk that day.

The next day, we drove further south and turned west at Dalrulzian to Pitlochry. I remembered from my last trip that the smallest distillery of Scotland was to be found near here: The Edradour. It was closed that time, and now seemed a good opportunity to visit it.

Edradour is a classic example of a distillery with adjoining farm. The staff consists of only three men. Edradour was founded in 1825 as a farmers' co-operative; the current buildings are from 1837 and were built by the Earl of Athol. Not much has changed in the past 160 years, except in 1947 when the water wheel was replaced by electricity.

Everything about Edradour is small: the cast-iron mash tun with a capacity of only 1 ton of barley, two washbacks made of Oregon pine, and two small stills. The stillhouse is the size of a living room and the spirit still has the smallest dimensions allowed, that is according to customs regulations. A smaller still could too easily be hidden in the hills. This region is known for its smuggling stories. The annual production of Edradour is also very small, about the same as the weekly production of an average Speyside distillery. The whisky is completely handcrafted, unique and hard to find, but worth the search. Its aroma is "as if you enter a sweetshop from the days of Dickens" to cite Graham Nown. The same can be said of the distillery.

The teachers from Friesland got a good look and they were surprised to find that distilleries could be so different. Wait till you see a big one, I thought. When I suggested we visit Glenfiddich to conclude our trip, they declined. They would rather spend more time enjoying the scenery. So I drove on, west, taking the A9, around the Grampian Mountains, Aviemore and the Cairngorms, to turn east again at Grantown-on-Spey and arrive at Corgarff Castle by way of the A939, through Lecht, a famous ski centre. We entered an area with many castles, all of them absolutely splendid. Just as distilleries mark the Speyside, castles mark the area around Aberdeen. We continued east on the A97 and the A944 and we passed GlenBuchat Castle, Kildrummy Castle and Castle Fraser before we returned to Aberdeen late in the afternoon. I had converted two more people to the beauty of the Scottish landscape and it gave me an idea to organise similar trips for other business relations. Short trips, both educational and hedonistic, replete with a study element so that the participants could have the taxman subsidise the travel expenses. Back in my hotel room, I immediately worked out the idea of 'package holidays'. It became the basis of various trips that I would undertake in the future with small groups of whisky and Scotland lovers.

The next day, we concluded our business with Aberdeen College and I flew back home with two brand new Scotland marketeers. It would not take long before I could celebrate a reunion with Roddy Scott and his crew.

Craigellachie
Friday, 2 May 2003, 3:00 pm

When I walk past the reception desk, Carol Brown, who has been part of the hard core of the staff for years, tells me there is someone in the games room waiting for me. I walk through the striking corridor with its red carpet and with paintings and portraits from the past adorning the walls. At the end, on the right, is a small, cosy room with a modestly sized snooker table. In one of the Morris chairs, next to the open fire – there is an open fire in each of the rooms on the ground floor, except for the bar – is a figure-head of the Scotch whisky industry: Wallace Milroy, gener-ally regarded as the first author to bring a taster's guide onto the market. The Malt Whisky Almanac – A Taster's Guide *was first published in 1986 and is now in its 7th edition. It has sold over 500,000 copies worldwide.*

We have known each other about three years thanks to Duncan Elphick, who, due to his never-ending efforts to promote the region, is also referred to as Mr Speyside. On November 11, 1998, I drank the one and only single malt still missing from the list in my almanac in the bar of the Craigellachie Hotel. Duncan wrote the following comment in my book: "Hans, a privilege to be with you on your completed volume I!"

It was not until early 2000, when I was in The Craig with a group of businessmen, that I understood what he meant by Volume I.

"Hi Hans, how are you," Wallace exclaims cheerily as he gets up from his chair to shake hands. He gestures at

the snooker table, gets a cue and points at a pint of beer that is waiting for me. Three frames later it's: Scotland-Netherlands 3-0, Wallace 3 beers, Hans 1. It is impossible to keep up with him as far as the drinking goes. I learned not to when we first met in person and I assisted at a whisky dinner. It was one of the few times that I have been drunk as a skunk.

Today, I take it easy or I will not make it through the night with Michael and Martine. Wallace suggests a walk and we leave the hotel to clamber through the garden down to the Speyside Way, which passes right in front of the hotel. The walk ends after only about ten minutes when we reach the Fiddichside Inn, the smallest pub of Scotland, run by Dorothy and Jim, both in their eighties. Dorothy is a colourful person who served in the Royal Air Force in World War II. She inherited the pub from her father and when she passes on it will probably mean the end of the Inn too, because it ceased to make money long ago.

The sun is shining brightly and we go outside to sit on a bench that has a view of the extremely well-kept garden and the River Fiddich, which meets the Spey a bit further on. Wallace, who is sometimes referred to as 'the walking liver', drinks one pint after another and treats me to all kinds of anecdotes from his illustrious whisky past. Time flies and as darkness falls we walk back to the hotel. A bit later, a taxi picks up Wallace and I go up to change for dinner, because I am expected to appear in Highland dress, in the kilt of my own clan.

Craigellachie and Auchentoshan
1997

The idea of organising whisky study trips was a good one. I tested the subject on friends and acquaintances and got enthusiastic reactions. The fact that I gave tastings at home no doubt influenced their reactions. I studied the organisational aspect and soon arrived at the conclusion that it would be smart to involve someone in Scotland who could make special arrangements for me, book accommodations and make deals. After all, I had no experience whatsoever with being a tour operator. When I cautiously approached Roddy Scott about the subject, his reaction was less than enthusiastic, mainly because he was too busy with the financial management of Aberdeen College. It was no use getting him involved.

In the meantime, the Scottish conversion of the two teachers from Friesland College had spread like wildfire and had reached other education circles in Friesland. At the end of March, a certain Rinze Boersma, director of the GCO (joint centre for education support) in Leeuwarden, called me and asked if I could meet with him to discuss new media in education. We set a date to meet in his office and I went to the capital of Friesland. We had hardly begun our meeting when Boersma asked me about my activities for Friesland College in relation to Scotland. He had also heard some very enthusiastic stories from the two teachers. I told him that I could introduce him to people at Aberdeen College, where they were using very modern audiovisual media. Boersma preferred to go on a trip with me and to reserve some time to get to know 'the Scots and their habits'.

Frankly, his request was made a little too early for me. I had not yet completely worked out the best way of organising a trip and to travel with one person for three or four days did not seem like a good start to me. However, Boersma wanted to know if I could arrange it in the very near future and how much it would cost. Out of politeness and because I did not want to decline at this point I gave him a ridiculously high price, expecting him to say no. Moreover, I had just planned my third trip with Rudolf, which was to take us to the Orkneys and the north coast of Scotland in May.

Boersma was indeed shocked at the price and said he wanted a week to think about it. After having exchanged a few ideas about educational innovation I left and went home. Four days later, his secretary called me to say we had a deal. This was not what I had intended to happen, but there was no turning back at this point. I called Roddy Scott for some travel tips and asked him when I could see him together with Boersma. At the end of April, he said, which was just over three weeks before my trip with Rudolf.

Boersma was very excited when I called him and a fortnight later we flew to Aberdeen on the morning flight. As usual, the people at Aberdeen College warmly welcomed us and Rinze Boersma was given ample opportunity to study the teaching materials and methods used by the College.

In the course of the afternoon, we left to go west. I took the A96 for a change, which leads to Inverness by way of Elgin. Roddy Scott had advised me to visit the ruins in Huntly. I drove on without much purpose while Rinze enjoyed the view. We stopped in Huntly to visit the magnificently restored ruins of the castle. When we drove off, I did not pay attention, and accidentally left the A96 and ended up on the A920. I noticed my mistake when I got to Dufftown, so I took the A941 north. Five minutes later I saw the sign for Craigellachie.

Seven years prior to this, I had also been in this village with the unpronounceable name when Rudolf and I had spent the night here. I kept my eyes peeled for the B&B Craigellachie Lodge sign, but because I now came from a different direction than seven years ago, I missed it. That's a shame, I thought, but I'll continue to Elgin. When I turned onto the A94 I saw a characteristic, white Victorian building in the corner of my eye. At that moment Rinze said: "That seems like a nice hotel to spend the night."

We turned right and soon after we stood on the crunching gravel of the Craigellachie Hotel of Speyside car park. The stone stairs in the corner led us to the entrance. We entered and I was completely sold. We walked into a 'timeless presence in an ever-changing world', which is oft-heard praise for the hotel. The lady at the reception desk introduced herself as Carol Brown. She checked the register and said she had two rooms left. I nodded and she poured us a whisky by way of welcome. Not in a glass, but in a traditional 'quaich'. Later I learned that the Scots used the quaich for their victory drinks. We were invited to go to the bar and hand over our car key. The luggage would be collected from the car and taken to our rooms. Rinze grumbled approvingly, "Not a bad job, Hans", which, coming from a Frisian, is a compliment.

As we toasted and had our first drink, a tall man with short, grey hair walked in.

"*Ceud mille failte*," my name is Duncan Elphick and I am the manager of the hotel. May I join you for a drink?"

He pulled up a chair, sat down and told us that he had been appointed director two weeks ago by the new owners, a group of Danish investors. They wanted to give the hotel, which had fallen somewhat into decline, a new image and they had decided to carry out a major renovation which would take a number of years.

"Currently not all the rooms are available, due to renovations," explained Elphick. "Apart from you two, the only other guests are a group of Danes, amongst whom two of the owners. The rest of the group are building and construction workers. Tonight there is a whisky tasting in the bar. Do you care to join?"

We happily agreed because it sounded like fun

"What are we drinking now?" I asked.

"Craigellachie, of course" Elphick replied.

I got out my little bible, ticked off Craigellachie, looked around the bar and saw an enormous number of bottles on the shelves on the wall. All single malts by the look of it. If there was a place where I could complete the collection of malts to be drunk, this was it.

"Okay then, we'll start at seven thirty. See you then, and please call me Duncan." And off he went, after a curious glance at the purple book I was holding.

That evening I learned what a smooth host Duncan was. Inviting us to the tasting was a smart move, because the Danes were noisy and our presence at the session made us accomplices. We lost all right to complain.

An older man, marketing manager at Glenlivet, presented the tasting. He introduced himself as Mark Lawson. A blended name for someone who aims to promote a single malt, I thought. He started telling the story of how whisky is produced, but the Danes weren't interested. They already had had one pint too many earlier that day.

Lawson soon realised it was a waste of time and moved on to presenting the first whisky, Auchentoshan, the archetypical Lowland malt. He looked in my direction and queried, "May I ask what you smell?"

I swirled the whisky and replied, "Light, delicate, some citrus and a hint of dried grass," after which I grabbed my book and took down some notes.

Startled and pleasantly surprised, he next turned to one of the Danes, "And what about you?"

"Id zmellz like fvisky," the fuddled Dane replied in fat tones, after which the entire group burst out laughing and mockingly looked in our direction. This group was clearly beyond tasting.

The next malts followed in rapid succession. The Danes wanted their dinner and disappeared half an hour later to the restaurant downstairs. Lawson came over to us and shook hands. He wanted to know where we were from and how it was possible that I had given him such a specific description of the Auchentoshan.

"First of all, I am not drunk" I started. Lawson hooted

with laughter and said, "Please call me Mark."

I then told him about the journey I had begun in 1974 and which had finally taken me to this bar, in 1997. Rinze listened, clearly enjoying the story, and ordered another dram. He was quickly acquiring a taste for all this, and happily relaxed in his chair while Mark and I engaged in an animated conversation. I understood that he had taken early retirement, but on occasions such as this one, sometimes was active for Seagram, the then-owner of Glenlivet. He was also involved in promoting the region and had been hired by the hotel to take care of the marketing.

I asked him a thousand questions about nosing and tasting, about a balanced choice, deciding on the best order and about the most effective way to captivate your audience. He gave me a couple of valuable tips. In the years to follow, he gave me many more. And thus, Mark Lawson became my third teacher, after Guy Laroche and Tom Douwma.

Rinze and I spent the rest of the evening in the restaurant because Mark had to return to Elgin, where he lived. The Danes, saturated by drink and food, had moved on to the library. After an excellent dinner, Duncan came over to ask if everything had been to our liking. He offered us a digestive in the shape of a 25-year-old Macallan. That night we slept undisturbed by the noisy fury of the Danes, and came down for breakfast feeling fairly bright. I noticed that everything had been meticulously taken care of and the staff were present in a pleasant way; never noticeably so, but always ready to serve. This was a hotel I had to show Rudolf.

Before I settled the bill at the reception desk, I asked Duncan if I could speak to him privately. He invited me into the library, while Rinze was packing his bag. I told Duncan about the two trips with my best friend, and asked him if he could book two rooms for three weeks later. I would lead Rudolf to Craigellachie as if by coincidence, on our way to the Orkneys, and pretend I had never been to the hotel before. As soon as we entered I would be greeted like an old friend and this would result in my friend being totally wrong-footed. Duncan liked the practical joke and promised to instruct his staff accordingly.

"See you in three weeks" he called out as we left the car park. The foundation for two friendships had been laid. Moreover, Mark and Duncan were right sort to actively help me in further developing the programme of my package trips. Two days later I delivered a completely satisfied Rinze Boersma to his family in Friesland.

Craigellachie

It is time to get ready for the whisky dinner. In full dress, I stride down the wooden stairs and go to the drawing room where I find Michael Jackson, together with Dave Broom, another whisky author and journalist, sitting on the sofa with a Newcastle Pale Ale and an Aberlour 10-year-old. Apart from being a fabulous whisky expert, Michael is also an authority on beer. When I met him, at the 2002 Festival, he surprised us by holding a combined beer/whisky tasting. It is remarkable to find that the right whisky can accompany the right beer and they each intensify the taste of the other drink. Quite different than the common Dutch version, called 'kopstoot', (Dutch jenever and beer). Michael earned the title of Baedeker of Booze in Great Britain, and rightly so. Dave is holding a nosing glass and intensively noses the contents, while Michael anxiously awaits his judgement. The two gentlemen sometimes have opposing views when it comes to nosing and tasting.

"I smell old, dead wood, mushrooms and damp leaves," Dave starts.

"That's not whisky, that's your moustache, Dave," is Michael's instant reaction.

"Sit down, sit down," says Michael and I grab a chair. Dave excuses himself. He is expected in Elgin to present a tasting. Immediately after he leaves, Hideo Yamaoka enters. This is a man I have great respect for. He managed to translate the Malt Whisky Companion *into Japanese*

and publish it. Last year, Michael gave me the 4th edition, and in it, he wrote a note asking me to translate the upcoming 5th edition into Dutch and publish it. Hideo is one of the guests tonight and a great lover of Springbank, the 21-year-old edition in particular. Not long ago, I was sitting at the Quaich bar with him, and he had a bottle of the precious stuff on a chain around his neck and he let anyone who wanted have a drink. It kept him from dropping the bottle, because our Japanese friend was not as steady on his feet as usual that evening.

He wants to hear about the menu in advance, but we prefer to have Martine reveal it. A bit later, feigning disappointment, he disappears in the direction of the bar no doubt. To please him, Michael has put a Springbank on the menu. When Martine Nouet enters a little while later, accompanied by Duncan Elphick, we sit down to study the seating arrangement and division of tasks. Four people, four nationalities, one fascination.

Glenfarclas, Glenmorangie, Highland Park and Scapa
1997

"Orkney, here we come!" is what Rudolf had written on the money transfer note that paid for the first part of the costs of our third trip. He did not know yet that we would make a minor detour after Ingliston. I had chosen to fly to Edinburgh because I wanted to drive to Craigellachie by way of the Grampians and because I had flown to Aberdeen three weeks earlier. To me, variation is one of the essential ingredients of life.

During our previous trips, we had developed a routine. Rudolf read the map and I drove. I had been to Scotland so many times now that reading the map was no longer necessary, at least not as far as Inverness, because I had not been north of that city yet. My friend could thus fully enjoy the scenery and did not notice that I was making a detour. We took the A93 passing Glenshee, a famous ski area, and stopped in Braemar for a cup of coffee in the same hotel where I had spent the night the year before with the Frisian teachers. This time, Balmoral Castle, a little further, was open and we decided to go in. The gardens are extremely appealing and you can walk there for hours, but the castle itself has very limited access to the public. It did not take us long to finish and continue our trip. I turned left at Crathie and took a terrific, small, curvy by-road (the B976) to get to the A939, which we followed until we reached Grantown-on-Spey.
There, we took the A95, which would take us to Craigellachie in less than thirty minutes.

Halfway, we passed Ballindalloch Castle, the owner of which owns the oldest herd of Aberdeen Angus in Great Britain. A few years later, I used the castle as the backdrop in a documentary for a commercial TV station. During the interview, the Countess told me proudly that she shared a bull with the queen mother who also owned an Angus herd in the far north of Scotland. Where does your pride lie?

That day, we preferred the right side of the road, because that's where Glenfarclas was, the only distillery from the original whisky trail that we had not visited in 1990. We wanted to set the record straight before we sailed to Orkney. Glenfarclas was bought by John Grant from the original owner, Robert Hay, shortly after it was founded in 1836 and since then it had stayed in the hands of this family. One of the few distilleries that did. In 1997, the wave of mergers rolled over Scotland, which resulted in most distilleries being owned by large conglomerates. The motto 'the spirit of independence' underscores the pride of the Grant family.

What made Glenfarclas extra special to us was the fact that it contained the largest stills in the Speyside. They were large indeed. We inhaled the characteristic aroma once again with great appreciation during the tour, which ended in the excellent visitor's centre, part of which had been boarded with the original oak panelling taken from the cruise ship *Empress of Australia* that sailed from 1913 until 1952. John L.S. Grant, the fifth generation of this dynasty, holds very particular views on marketing. He happened to be there and welcomed us warmly, poured us a dram and had one too. After we had both bought a miniature, we thanked him and left. The evening drew near and I had let Duncan Elphick know that we would arrive around six in the evening, so that his people would be ready for us.

Craigellachie can be reached from three directions: east, south and north. We entered the village from Aberlour, from the south. When you turn right into the village, you suddenly see the hotel in full glory. I casually remarked that I was a bit tired and would like to call it a day. I pointed at the hotel.

"That looks okay, doesn't it?"

Rudolf nodded approvingly. Seven years ago, we had to travel on a fairly low budget, but in 1997 he was an established dentist and I earned a good living from my media consultancy and my writing. The time of small B&Bs was behind us. When I entered the car park and heard the gravel crunch under the wheels, I said to myself: 'déjà écouté!'

"Do you think they will have rooms left?" Rudolf asked unsuspectingly.

"I hope so, let's ask them first."

Without our suitcases, we climbed the steps now familiar to me. I held open the door for my friend who slowly entered the magnificent hall, feasting his eyes on the things around him. Slightly hesitantly, he walked over to the reception desk, where Carol was writing something. She did not respond to Rudolf immediately and he just stood there waiting until she was done.

Suddenly, from the library, a smiling, tall man came walking towards us. Rudolf prepared to shake hands, but the man passed straight by him and called out, "Well

Hans, how good to see you again. Welcome, can I offer you the same dram you had last time?"

Rudolf was flabbergasted but only for a minute; he immediately recovered and said, "The same for me please!"

Carol got up and showed Rudolf what she had done: she had filled in his details on a registration form.

"You have quite a bit of explaining to do, mate," he said and I waved him into the bar.

"Take a look at this. So many whiskies in one place!"

Rudolf was very impressed by the enormous collection of single malts, as I had been three weeks earlier.

"We've six more than last time," said the barkeeper as we sat down on one of the sofas. I picked up a ring binder with tasting notes and showed Rudolf what Rinze Boersma and I had drunk with the Danes. A while later, Duncan joined us carrying three glasses of Craigellachie.

"These anecdotes will build the myth around the hotel," he chuckled. Just how serious he was, I would find out that evening.

That night, after dinner, we played a couple of games of snooker in the games room and went to the library for a nightcap. Duncan joined us again. He wanted to know how Rudolf liked the hotel and how my previous guest had liked it. I unfolded my plans for business trips and he was on the edge of his seat. What if the hotel were to become the focal point of these trips? Duncan had several relevant contacts in the region and could organise a good package and arrange things on the spot and in advance. Just what I needed. Rudolf was tired and

The road to Craigellachie

went to bed. We explored all the things we could do to put the hotel on the map until the early hours of the morning. It wasn't just the unique whisky collection and the enormous stock of rare malts in the cellar, but also the central location that made The Craig perfect as the starting point for exploring the Speyside and adjacent regions. We drew up a list of activities that could make up a package:

> *visit to a distillery,*
> *trout fishing,*
> *salmon fishing,*
> *hunting,*
> *clay pigeon shooting,*
> *quad biking and off-road driving,*
> *nosing & tasting,*
> *visit to Loch Ness (a one-hour-and-a-half's drive),*
> *castles (Ballindalloch, Brodie, Cawdor, Fyvie to*
> *list a few in the neighbourhood).*

As soon as I was back in the Netherlands, I would take inventory in my circle of friends and acquaintances to assess the most popular activities and I would mail the results to Duncan. He would compile packages, from which I could choose. Filled with these great plans, we left the library at four in the morning.

Later that morning, at breakfast, I excitedly told Rudolf about all the things I was planning to do. He smiled slightly unbelievingly, as always a little sceptical about my new undertakings, but always willing to pay me compliments whenever I actually managed to get things off the ground. Rudolf is a friend who shows me my shortcomings but happily gives me credit for my successes.

After having been sent off by Carol and Duncan, we continued on our way north. We wanted to spend the night in John O'Groats, Scotland's Land's End, in the far northeastern point of the mainland. Past Inverness, Rudolf picked up the map and guided me to Tain, home of Glenmorangie, by way of the A9. This was a distillery he was eager to visit because, in his university days, a fellow-student of his had been addicted to this single malt. Glenmorangie is Gaelic for 'valley of tranquility' and we confirmed this during our visit. The stills have the longest necks in the industry and are called 'swan's necks'. The malt is also known for the fact that since 1995 a series of special wood-finishes has been brought onto the market. After the tour, we were given a sherry, a port and a Madeira-wood to taste. I just took a sip because we still had a long way to go.

The A9 led us north by way of the coast. The road meanders and curves like no other, and it took us much longer to reach our destination than I had anticipated. We arrived at John O'Groats in the evening, and slept in the octagonal house that Jan de Groot – a Dutchman who had ended up in Scotland in the 19th century – had built. He had seven sons and in those tumultuous days it was important to always be close to the door so you could escape in case strangers with bad intentions arrived. That is why he had a door in every wall, so that they could all run out simultaneously in case of danger. Legend has it that the table they used also had eight sides, because they all wanted to sit at the head of the table. In this part of Scotland folklore abounded, just like we had come across in 1995 on the west coast, when we attended a ceilidh on the Isle of Skye. Sitting around the fire, we were told many more exciting stories from times past by the innkeeper. After he heard we wanted to sail to the Orkneys, he warned us.

"Strange people, those Orcadians. Neither Scots nor Norse."

With this warning in mind, we went to bed and got up very early the next morning to drive to Scrabster from where the car ferry left for Mainland, the largest of the Orkney Isles. The crossing took a couple of hours and we were lucky with the weather, because the seas can be very rough here, or so we had been told the night before. We passed the first island with its famous straight rock pinnacle called the Old Man of Hoy. We landed in Stromness and drove on to Kirkwall, the capital. Signs led us to Highland Park, the main goal of our journey. We wanted to add this whisky distillery - the most northerly in Scotland - to our list. According to local lore, the distillery was founded at the end of the 18th century by Magnus Eunson, one of the many smugglers and whisky distillers who protested against the high taxes imposed on them to pay for the war with France. It was said that Eunson used his position as verger to hide whisky in the pulpit!

This story was a good reason for us to visit St Magnus Cathedral after our tour of the distillery. The cathedral is an 11th century red brick, impressive Roman church, which according to history, had been built by the Norwegians. In centuries past, this group of islands regularly changed hands between the Norwegians and the Danes until a Danish princess was married off to a Scottish nobleman and the Orkneys were made part of the dowry.

That marked the end of alternating ownership of the islands. However, the inhabitants still boast about the fact that they are descendants of the Vikings and they feel closer to Scandinavia than to Scotland.

Armed with fine-looking Highland Park sweaters made of Shetland wool, which we had bought in the distillery shop, we further explored Mainland. The Orkneys are littered with prehistoric remains and we visited the Ring of Brodgar (Orkney's own Stonehenge, but smaller), the Standing Stones of Stennes and the prehistoric village of Skara Brae, the oldest, still intact human settlement in Western Europe. This village was laid bare by accident in 1840 after a tremendous storm blew away most of the sand that covered Skara Brae. We could really tell from the way the village has been conserved how people must have lived 5,000 years ago.

I had read in a flyer that there was a tomb on the southernmost island, South Ronaldsay, and I simply had to see it. In the afternoon, via the Churchill Barriers that connect the islands, we drove to the Tomb of the Eagles located on the land of a farmer. In the fifties, he had personally excavated some sites that were so sensational that a delegation from the British Museum arrived on the island not long after to continue the excavations professionally and take a large portion of the objects they found back to the mainland of Great Britain. All this infuriated the farmer of course who was only allowed to keep a small part. He personally gave us a tour of his land and he let me pull myself into the Tomb, stretched out on a trolley, through a tiny corridor, which was no more than 70 centimetres high. The corridor was longer than I had expected and when I was inside, surrounded by inky darkness, I was suddenly terror-stricken. The farmer had told me there was a light switch inside, but I was still very apprehensive. I slowly pulled myself in further using the ceiling. A bit later I felt the ceiling disappear and, as instructed by the farmer, I felt around the corner with my right hand and found a switch. As soon as I had turned on the light, five age-old skulls were staring me in the face, grinning. The idea that Rudolf was waiting for me outside suddenly seemed a very comforting thought.

"You should go too," I bravely called out to him, turned the trolley around, switched off the light and towed myself outside. The farmer stood there laughing, and said, "Ah, we're Orcadians, after all", after which Rudolf went through the same ordeal.

Slightly subdued, we drove back with the farmer to his cottage where he wanted to show us a glass case with some of the objects he had dug up. He opened the glass door, took out another skull and almost threw it to me. I dared not drop it, catching it firmly.

"That's what a 5,000-year-old skull feels like," he chuckled.

In Rudolf's case, his profession kicked in. He studied the skull extensively and concluded that the man had died of a vicious infection of the jaw. That made the tension disappear. What also helped was the dram of whisky the farmer offered to make ammends for playing his joke on us.

"Here, try this one. It's the other Orkney malt, Scapa."

With warmed hearts and bellies we left the farmer's land and stopped at St Margaret's Hope where we found a roof for the night in the Creel Inn. The owner of the tiny restaurant worked his magic in the kitchen and we treated ourselves to fish that had been caught in the bay that very morning. When I looked out the window of my room the next day, I saw the bay, lying there peacefully.

There are hardly any trees on Orkney. You don't really miss them because the pattern painted by the coast, the water, and the sky in all shades of green, white and blue is a feast to the eye.

After our adventure in the Tomb of the Eagles we of course had to visit Scapa before we could leave the Orkneys. The distillery was closed or 'moth-balled' as they say in the industry, which unfortunately happened regularly. Scapa is a nice after-dinner malt with tones of chocolate in the nose; it is very different from Highland Park, which is not even a mile away.

At the gate, we were welcomed by an old fellow named David Reed. He introduced himself as 'the last wash-man' and told us he checked the grounds every day. There was still a lot of whisky maturing in cask, worth a considerable sum of money, and he predicted that the 12-year-old would soon come onto the market. He let us walk the grounds with him and, inside, he only showed us the reception area with the showcase. As a token of appreciation for our interest, he gave us both a miniature for our collection. Rudolf took a picture of him in front of the showcase while I signed the register. I would send him a print of the photo when we got back to the Netherlands.

We rushed back to Stromness to catch the ferry to the mainland. Our adventure on Orkney had come to an end. In front of us was the virgin north Scottish coast waiting quietly.

Craigellachie
Friday, 2 May 2003, 8:00 pm

One by one, the guests are entering the Avon Room and looking for their place at the table. Duncan welcomes each and every one of them. This is a truly cosmopolitan group of 36 people, divided over four tables, across languages and borders, bound by one fascination.

Michael starts by giving an introduction and explains how Martine and he arrived at the choice of malts and dishes. The menu is an excellent one; it only has local dishes, ranging from shellfish and fish to lamb, venison and the ubiquitous haggis. During dinner, a lively discussion develops about the how and why of Talisker with oysters, Aberlour with venison and haggis with Glenfarclas. Here too, the cliché holds that there is no accounting for tastes. I write down some especially adventurous combinations that I pick up from the Norwegian sitting across from me who insists that Bowmore is undrinkable. I will use these notes when I get back to the Netherlands. A friend of mine has a cooking studio and together we organise whisky tastings with matching finger-foods. Thanks to Martine, tonight I discover how good Lagavulin tastes when it is combined with a cup of Lapsang Souchong tea.

The Norwegian still insists that you cannot drink Bowmore, and I challenge him to try the 17-year-old after dinner in the Quaich Bar. Dessert consists of Scottish cheeses presented with a 30-year-old Balvenie Portwood finish. Beautifully rich, with a silky taste, and with much more character than the Glenmorangie Portwood.

After dessert, Michael and Martine give every guest a signed copy of their books, the Companion *and* Les Routes du Malt. *I beckon the Norwegian to come to the bar and ask the barkeeper for a Bowmore 17. My companion noses, tastes, sits down and says, "This is not Bowmore, this is delicious." The barkeeper smiles and puts the bottle on the counter with the label facing the Norwegian.*

"Well Bowmore it is, I surrender," says the Norwegian, being a great sport, and he offers me a Highland Park 18-year-old, the whisky he liked best at dinner. It turns into another late night. One day to go, and the Festival will be over. With the taste of Highland Park still on my lips, I go to bed and dream of northern Scotland.

Laphroaig and Glenglassaugh
1997

Our journey along the north coast was an unforgettable
one. Splendid, quiet and spotless beaches. Magnificent
views with ever-changing skies, rocks of over two billion
years old, hardly marked, and almost no people.

We drove on in complete silence, each of us happy to be
thinking our own thoughts. The Orkney impressions also
needed to be processed. I stopped at regular intervals
to take pictures. It would turn out to be the best series I
had ever made in Scotland. We had four days to go and
decided to spend the night in this earthly paradise; we
counted on finding a hotel on the most northwesterly
point. Indeed, a white building took shape: Cape Wrath
Hotel. It reminded me of Rudolf's town, Gramsbergen,
a very similar name when translated, so this wasn't a
coincidence. It was a fisherman's hotel and thus soberly
decorated, but it provided the most beautiful view in all
of northern Scotland, at least in our opinion at the time.
I got my camera out and felt I was about to take a great
picture. Silent, and impressed by the natural beauty and
peace of the place, we ate a simple meal and went to bed
early.

The next day, we had an early start. The route took us
again through a breathtakingly beautiful landscape.

The A894 led to Loch Assynth. There was not a breath
of wind and the pictures I took showed the completely
unruffled reflections of the trees in the water. We drove
along the west side of Loch Ness, passing Ullapool and

Inverness, heading south on the A82, and then past Fort William and through Glen Coe, an elongated and narrow valley with sheer cliffs on the sides, which left us with an eerie feeling. I was glad to see the end of it and to arrive at the open spaces of Rannoch Moor. At Crianlarich, we turned left to pass Callander and then on to Edinburgh where we planned to spend two days getting to know the city better. At Lochearnhead I saw a sign for St Fillans and I suddenly remembered our adventure with the Golden Girls on Islay. I stopped at the crossing and said to Rudolf, "See that? Isn't that where Ulla Ross has her B&B? Shall we have a look?"

"Why not?" replied Rudolf and I turned the car left. The road meandered for five miles along Loch Earn before we entered St Fillans, a village with fewer than 300 inhabitants. At the end of the village, just past the loch, we saw a sign saying 'Earngrove Cottage, B&B'.

"This should be it," I said, and parked the car beside the road. We got out and walked to the front door. On top of the portal of the house, a Swedish and a Scottish flag were flying in harmony. I rang the bell.

"Do you think Ulla will remember us? It is two years ago after all," Rudolf wondered.

He had hardly finished his sentence when the door opened and there was Ulla,

"Hello Hans, hello Rudolf, how nice of you to drop by," she greeted us as if she had run into us at the supermarket last week.

"Meet my husband William."

From behind her, a sturdy Scot with bright white hair and a ruddy face appeared.

The north coast.

"So you are the lads from Islay. Ulla told me all about it when she got home. Come in."

He stuck out his hand and when I took it, his steel-blue eyes gave me a penetrating look. At that moment something unexplainable happened, as if miles and ages had been overcome. We both noticed it. It felt as if we got an electric shock. Rudolf was following Ulla into the small, cosy living room and sat down. William and I slowly followed suit, and we were both a little shaken. As soon as we were seated, Ulla entered with four glasses of whisky.

"Laphroaig," she smiled.

"Slainte," said William and we held up our glasses. There were no other guests and we both got a room for the night.

While Ulla and Rudolf reminisced about Islay, William and I kept staring at each other. There was something there, a mutual attraction that went beyond normal comprehension.

"Where did you come from?" William asked, breaking the silence.

I told him about Orkney and the north. About the energy emanating from the north coast. He noticed that I was still impressed. When I reached Glen Coe in my story, he interrupted with an anecdote about the betrayal of the Campbell Clan, which at the end of the 17th century, had slaughtered the MacDonalds as if it were a military operation, as a thank you for their fortnight of offering hospitality. No wonder I had found it an eerie place and it struck me again how deeply the Scots are rooted in their own history.

"A Ross would never do that. Never mix with a Campbell, son," said William, completing his story. He pulled a small booklet about the history of his clan off the bookshelf and showed me the names of famous people brought forth by Clan Ross. I went through the list and came across Sir James Clark Ross, who had discovered the magnetic north pole in 1831, and I saw that Ronald Ross had won the Nobel Prize in 1902 because he had proven that there is a connection between mosquitoes and malaria. So I was in good company. Still, that did not explain our sudden connection.

"You seem a son of the country. I can tell you feel at home here and are susceptible to the atmosphere. Old head on young shoulders we say. You must have had a past life in Scotland, that's for sure."

Any other time, I would have found this slightly too mystical for my taste, but coming from a tough Scot, who had been a professional army man, policeman and hotel owner in Edinburgh before he retired, I was ready to accept it.

"Welcome to the Ross-clan," said William and he gave me the booklet and a key ring with the arms and motto of the clan: *Spem successus alit.*

"Success nourishes hope," he explained.

At that moment, he became my spiritual father, even though I did not really know this until I got back to the Netherlands.

Rudolf and Ulla were having a whale of a time and the moment, which was so special to me, seemed to have passed unnoticed by my friend. Rudolf invited us to a pub meal in the Achray Inn, a hotel a little ways back, that we had noticed when we entered St Fillans.

The four of us walked past the loch to the Achray. While seated, I told Bill (William had asked us to call him that) and Ulla how I had become so attached to whisky and Scotland. Rudolf sat listening and nodded every now and then to confirm an anecdote from our previous trips. When we walked back after dinner, we were completely fraternised, and this was the result of the stories rather than the whisky. Rudolf went to bed early. I stayed up for a long time talking to Bill and Ulla and I increasingly felt as if I was with my parents.

The next morning, I drove off in a low mood, after I had hugged them both for a long time. Rudolf shrugged his shoulders. He had had a good time with them, but he was not susceptible to that kind of emotion.

"Cheer up, you will see them again soon. At the rate you're going, visiting this country, you don't have to worry about that." They proved to be prophetic words.

When we arrived in Edinburgh, we drove to Leith, the old harbour, to spend the night in one of the flats that the Scotch Malt Whisky Society (or the SMWS) makes available to its members. They were located in an old warehouse that had been restored in a fine manner when the city decided to give this run-down part of Edinburgh a facelift. In the warehouse there was a beautiful member's club where all bottled whiskies could be tasted. Some years ago, Rudolf and I had become members of this illustrious club that buys its casks directly from the distilleries and bottles the whisky in numbered bottles. The advantage of being a member was mainly that you could order very special editions that were not available in shops and thus surprise your friends with an exclusive dram. I ordered a fairly rare Glenglassaugh, light and delicate, with a stimulating aftertaste, after which I ticked off one more item in Wallace's almanac. In the Netherlands, I often use the SMWS malts at a tasting for experienced whisky drinkers. The club gave us a fine finale to our third trip, the most eventful one so far. Due to our spontaneous visit to St Fillans, we had no time left to explore the city and we flew back to the Netherlands the next morning. Rudolf went back to work. I needed a week to process my impressions, and an extra week in which I wrote down what I had experienced, thus unintentionally laying the foundations for this book. From that time on, I was no longer sure if I belonged in the Netherlands or in Scotland.

Craigellachie
Saturday, 3 May 2003, 10:00 am

After last night's lavish dinner, nobody wants to get up early. Even at 10 am, I am one of the few early birds in the breakfast room. I have an appointment at 11 with John Grant of Glenfarclas, so I have to be up. The taxi takes me to the 'valley of green grass', which is how the Gaelic name translates.

John is waiting for me in his office, surrounded by paraphernalia from the past. If there is one distillery that has documented its heritage to a T, it is this one. The door opposite John's desk leads to his private lab that holds scores of sample bottles. The owner himself sometimes also engages in blending. John takes out of a cupboard the oldest existing bottle of Glenfarclas, from the end of the 19th century. He proudly shows it to me and I take a picture. We sit down comfortably because I have promised to interview him for a food & drink magazine published in the Netherlands. I don't have to ask many questions. Across from me is a noted raconteur who coughs up one anecdote after another.

To illustrate his stories and emphasise their authenticity, John opens drawer after drawer to take out pieces of evidence. A note from Margaret Thatcher from 1989, in which she thanks him for the bottles of Glenfarclas 15-year-old that she received after a visit to the distillery. John relates, "I told her during her visit that it had come to our attention that the tenant of Downing Street 10 did not support the British industry, serving cognac when whisky would've been more appropriate. She apologised and after that only drank our 15-year-old." I don't know if the last part is true, but it's the stuff the Glenfarclas myth is built on.

Kenneth Clark, Chancellor of the Exchequer in 1994, has his own cask here. Michael Schumacher came by on his motorcycle a few years ago, but was only recognised by the staff when they saw him on TV. Until 1990, there was a herd of Aberdeen Angus in the fields surrounding the distillery that was the oldest-but-one in the world. The pedigree makes a mention of Percy, the champion bull of Glenfarclas in 1968.

Going abroad is something Glenfarclas has been doing for a long time. In reply to my question if they also buy barley from places other than Scotland, John said, "Of course, wherever we can get the best bargain for the best quality."

He digs up yet another anecdote from his memory. In the times before the EC, he regularly bought outside of Europe. He once got offered fine barley at a great price in Adelaide and immediately decided to order 600 tons and wrote on the form that the order had to be delivered in Buckie, Scotland. "When the barley arrived, I was very happy with the quality, but shocked by the price. I didn't realise transport costs from Australia to Scotland were added," he grins and pours me another cup of coffee.

The distillery itself has been adapted to the modern era of producing whisky and the layout looks modern. When I say something about that, John shakes his head and points to the pagoda on the roof of the visitor's centre, "1896, Charles Doig's first or second pagoda ever."

Time flies and after two hours I have enough material and pictures for an article. After I have given my greetings to Ishbel, John's wife, I let myself be driven back to The Craig, contented and still relishing all that I have just heard. I have known John Grant about five years now, and at each and every meeting he feeds me new particulars. On the way to The Craig, I reminisce about the first time we met.

Royal Brackla and Glenury Royal
1998

After our last trip, I was certain about one thing: from that moment on, I would live in two worlds. From the Netherlands, I kept up my Scottish contacts through e-mail and started looking for opportunities to combine work and pleasure as much as possible. The bond with William Ross became increasingly closer. A father without a son and a son without a father (my own father had died fairly suddenly in 1995) had found each other. We wrote each other many letters, and whenever I had to go to Scotland I always flew via Edinburgh or Glasgow and reserved the first day and night for a visit to Bill and Ulla, usually arriving with a bottle of single malt as a gift.

I also kept in close contact with Mark Lawson and we saw each other several times in The Craig in 1998. In the Netherlands, I was busy publishing books on demand, a procedure in which Mark was very interested. I liked being able to provide him with stories from my business in return for his whisky lessons. One day he asked me if the on-demand publishing method could also be applied to labels. I explained that theoretically the principle was applicable to any kind of publication, to which he responded with an exceptional story from the days he was still working at Glenlivet.

In that period, as the marketing manager at Glenlivet, he had had a say in the packaging and presentation of the product. Glenlivet used a designer and packaging specialist for this part of the process. The designer was a slightly peculiar and rather cocky man with the French-sounding name of LaDell.

"Nowadays he is retired and living in Moscow," said Mark. I looked at him, surprised, and he laughed and took out the map of Scotland to indicate a tiny village south of Glasgow.

"Moscow, Scotland, Hans."

"Of course Mark, please forgive a Dutchman his ignorance regarding Scottish geography."

Mark continued his story. John LaDell had been a phenomenon in the industry during his working life, had designed many a packaging and travelled around the world to advise other distillers, among whom the Japanese. He had developed the habit of writing to distilleries whenever a new brand or label was brought onto the market, asking for an unused copy. In the tens of years he had been doing this, he had built up a collection of thousands of whisky labels that is beyond compare. His dream was to have this collection published as a book.

During Mark's story, Duncan Elphick came in, and he heard the last bit. He was immediately interested in finding out whether we could do something with this unique collection to further establish the reputation of the hotel. I suggested that we turn it into a loose-leaf encyclopaedia and call it *The Craigellachie Collection of Scotch Whisky Labels*. Through the Internet, we could reach whisky lovers around the world and the hotel could function as the binding factor. Duncan and Mark were both game and we toasted the idea with a glass of Royal Brackla. When I ticked off this complex malt, smoky, dry and with a hint of fruit, in my little bible, both gentlemen leaned over and asked to have a look. I told them how I had come by it a couple of years back, how Wallace Milroy's *Almanac* had become my trusted companion since then, and about my self-imposed quest to try them all.

"You've done a great job so far. Not too many left I see," Mark said approvingly.

"You'll probably complete it here," Duncan added.

Mark promised to sound out John LaDell and think about a marketing plan. Duncan said he would ask the web designer of www.craigellachie.com for a quotation for a website that would enable people to place orders and, back in the Netherlands, I focused on production methods and means.

I returned to Craigellachie, on 7 November 1998, armed with a production plan, to meet John LaDell who had reacted quite enthusiastically to Mark's phone call. Duncan had asked The Vikings if they were interested in participating. 'Chief' Sören Gabriel had told me that he did not see the point. He did not object however to our using the name for the collection, not being averse to free publicity.

Surrounded by an enormous pile of albums with labels, the four of us founded a tiny Scottish publishing house in the library of The Craig. My heart skipped a beat. Now, I also had a company in Scotland! It turned into a historic event in many ways; I only had one more malt to go to complete the list in my bible: Glenury Royal, the last of the royal threesome Glenury, Brackla and Lochnagar.

"This is the bloody end," wrote John on page 86 of my book.

"Hans, a privilege to be with you on your completed volume I!" wrote Duncan.

Mark just sat there; he smiled and approved. He picked up a pile of papers and explained his marketing plan. It was important that we involve the distilleries because they would have to give permission for the publication of their labels. John said he had been given permission by a number of distilleries, but the rest of them still had to be visited or sent a request. We drew up a to-do-list and I imagined myself touring the country, going from distillery to distillery, work and fun going hand in hand. We left the library in a euphoric mood and had a dram in the Quaich Bar. In the corner, opposite the bar, was a couple. The man got up and introduced himself, "Enchanted, John Grant, nice to meet you. This is my wife Ishbel. By the way, it's my birthday, so have a dram of her favourite, the 15-year-old."

"Meet the owner of Glenfarclas," Duncan said to me. We joined them and told them about our plans. The whisky baron was immediately interested in the whisky label encyclopaedia and ordered one even before the first page had been produced.

"Please visit me tomorrow. I'll show you some nice labels that you can use," John Grant said to me when he said goodbye, many hours and drams later.

Craigellachie
Saturday, 3 May 2003, 1:00 pm

I return to the hotel around lunchtime. Most Speyside Festival attendees are on the road somewhere, on their way to a blending, a lecture, a distillery or to the estate of Innes McPherson, to go quad biking, trout fishing or clay pigeon shooting.

Duncan and I have time to do our own thing and we study a few new ideas for travel packages in the region. Since I was appointed 'Craigellachie Consul for the Netherlands' in 1999, I have referred many Dutchmen, Germans and Belgians to The Craig, sometimes tempting them with the promise of a dram from my bottle upon arrival. This has led to hilarious moments at times. The people at the hotel know that I will send them an e-mail in advance whenever a guest is on his or her way to whom I have promised a dram. Sometimes there is a mix up, especially in cases where the guest does not tell me when he or she expects to arrive at The Craig.

A couple of years ago, my brother called me late at night with a story that there was a furious Dutchman, whose name will remain undisclosed, in the Quaich Bar. He had tried everything to get a free dram from my bottle, had then called everyone by the name of Offringa in the Netherlands, spending a fortune in moibile phone charges, to end up calling my brother. The barkeeper kept refusing and the man was made a fool of in the face of the company he had meant to impress. My brother promised him I would call him at the hotel.

Never kick a man when he is down, so I called The Craig in the middle of the night and rescued him from the impossible situation. Relieved, and with a brief 'thank you', he hung up and, I assume, went back to the bar to render his audience speechless.

Duncan has some problems with the prices, especially for plane tickets. We have tried before to organise all-inclusive trips, but it didn't work. "We're not a f... tour-operator," says Duncan paraphrasing Sören Gabriel's infamous comment. The hotel cannot run the risk of booking plane seats and not selling them. The easiest flight from Amsterdam is the one to Aberdeen. However, the high rates that are charged for this KLM-dominated route make it more appealing to fly with Easyjet to Glasgow or Edinburgh, then rent a car and drive to The Craig. I prefer that route, because it takes you through wonderful country, and gives you ample opportunity to take different roads. We could set up a broader package than The Craig, for instance by including a stopover in a hotel half-way for the first night. That would however lead to all kinds of logistic and administrative obstacles because the hotel reservations systems are not compatible. Moreover, Duncan would rather have these guests stay at his hotel.

We have had the same problem with distilleries. Whereas most travellers like to drink different brands of whisky, the distilleries are not inclined to cooperate, unless they are part of the same conglomerate, like the Classic Malts Series of Diageo. I noticed the same thing with the marketing of John LaDell's whisky label encyclopaedia.

I find a well-thumbed copy on the buffet in the Spey room and my mind starts to wander.

Glenturret and Aberfeldy
1999

The year 1999 was the year of the encyclopaedia. I travelled to Scotland almost every month to spend a week or longer visiting as many distilleries as possible. I found my home away from home with Bill and Ulla, so Earngrove Cottage in St Fillans became my permanent base. When Ulla fell seriously ill, Bill and I comforted each other. I travelled during the day, and I could be found in that small village on Loch Earn at night. We talked about the past, present and future for many hours, and about life's main themes, things I had never been able to discuss with my biological father. And always, the talks were accompanied by a glass of Islay whisky, the island where I had met Ulla.

St Fillans is not too far from Moscow, where I went often to discuss progress with John and to collect new labels that had to be scanned and edited in the Netherlands. John delivered the texts, which were subsequently edited by Mark Lawson and me. The work I did may have seemed a courier's job, but it did not feel that way. Every day, I thoroughly enjoyed the travelling, the writing and the conversations with Bill.

The compilation of the encyclopaedia steadily progressed and it gave me an opportunity to call on distilleries I had not visited before.

One of them was Glenturret, near Crieff, about a 20-minute drive to the east of St Fillans. It was a beautifully old – the oldest according to the owner – small distillery with a remarkable inhabitant. Most distilleries have cats on the grounds. The animals like the heat of the stills and the distillers appreciate the fact that they catch the mice that are attracted by the barley. The cats are usually called Malt, Dram or Barley. Not so the famous house cat of Glenturret. She was called Towser the Mouser. In the 24 years of her life, this tortoiseshell cat had caught about 28,000 mice, which comes down to an average of over three a day. Her boss, one of the employees at Glenturret, for years had been taking notes every time his cat turned up with a mouse. This gained the cat an entry in the Guinness Book of World Records. During the tour, I saw a bronze statue of the famous cat on the distillery's courtyard. I found another trace of the cat on the Fairlees label, Glenturret's whisky liqueur. It looked as if a cat had walked over the galley proofs. These were perfect illustrations for our encyclopaedia.

Whenever Ulla had to go to the hospital for tests, Bill could spend the day with me. The first distillery I visited together with my Scottish faither was Aberfeldy, an hour north of St Fillans. The distillery was located just outside the village and the single malt is the heart of Dewar's blends. What also interested me was the history of the logo on the bottle, a squirrel. One of the previous managers really liked the species and had let loose a small colony of red squirrels in the woods behind the warehouses; they multiplied in no time. The manager's successor was not interested in the colony and the story faded out. So did the squirrels. But it gave me another fine anecdote for the encyclopaedia. Behind the distillery, I took a picture of the path that was to encourage the traveller to

The most famous cat in Scotland's distilling history.

check out the squirrels, and then we got back in the car and continued on our route. We made a long trip to the far northwest that day. I really wanted to show Bill the place where I had taken such a great picture the year before. When we returned home, after a fourteen-hour trip over great by-roads, Ulla was already home with good news. Her illness was under control and the prognosis was good. Our bond grew stronger and stronger.

To have easy access to the distilleries further north, I set up base camp at The Craig where we developed yet another idea one night, which was put into practice then and there: The Friends of Craigellachie Malt Whisky Club. Future members would be given privileges in the hotel, among which the space for their own bottle under lock and key, and a subscription to our whisky label collection. On April 15, the club was officially founded, consisting of two members: Duncan Elphick and the author of this book. A few years later, the club comprised 48 people from all over the world. The maximum number because we wanted it to remain an exclusive club. Now, there is a waiting list of at least 20 people. Whenever one of the current members decides to resign, he or she will sell his or her membership to the hotel, after which number one on the waiting list will be offered membership. Duncan offered me the first spot as a thank you for the idea.

By the end of 1999, I had collected all the material needed for the encyclopaedia and the majority of labels had been digitised. John LaDell indeed proved as stubborn as Mark had told me. He had not been active in the industry for many years and he was out of touch with current reality. This did not keep him from writing pages and pages of prose that proved less than accurate. It took Mark and me a great deal of time to check and adapt all these texts. The advantage was that I learned a lot about the whisky industry. The disadvantage was that our publishing project was becoming extremely expensive and the group of subscribers was not yet large enough to make the publication a cost-effective one.

Craigellachie
Saturday, 3 May 2003, from 2:00 pm onwards

Duncan looks up and notices me browsing through the whisky label encyclopaedia. With a note of pity he says, "Some things work, some don't." I sigh, put down the book and look at the new brochure Duncan has had made. It looks professional and beautiful. Some years ago, Mark Lawson still took care of the PR and all printed materials, but now, Duncan does most of that together with an advertising agency in Buckie. One of the founders, Lesley Ann Parker, is also closely involved in the organisation of the Speyside Festival.

"Let's play some snooker," my tall, grey-haired friend says. We walk to the games room and a little later, the barkeeper brings us both a beer. After five frames, Duncan and I collect his spaniels and take a short walk along the River Spey, towards Dufftown. At the Speyside Cooperage, Duncan turns around and walks back. I stay to take a few pictures and to greet some old friends. About an hour later, I walk back to the hotel alone, and enter the bar around 7:00 pm.

It is quite busy, cosy and warm there. My new Norwegian Bowmore friend calls me over and I join him. He wants to know what it is that I do, apart from organising whisky nosing & tastings. When I tell him I earn a large part of my living by writing, he shifts in his seat, and says: "Never write I didn't like Bowmore!"

I promise him I will not mention his name, but I may use the anecdote itself one day.

"What's on for tonight?" he asks.

"Ghost hunt at The Macallan," says the barkeeper.

"First let's eat," I say and get up to go to the restaurant downstairs. The Norwegian and his wife follow. They join me at the table. She paints and wants to know what I think of her work. She takes a couple of postcards from her purse, mini reproductions of the originals. It is a fresh, Scandinavian style. Mr Bowmore proudly shows me pictures of his whisky cabinet, back home in Oslo. It is an impressive collection.

"You don't drink them?" I ask.

"Oh, yes," his wife sighs. "He always buys two bottles, one for drinking and one for collecting!"

I make no comment and humbly stick my fork in the fresh salmon on my plate. I prefer to collect anecdotes.

The Macallan 30-year-old
2000

Early 2000, I returned with the galley proofs to The Craig to check the first results together with Mark, John and Duncan. John was impressed with the quality of the printed labels and carefully compared them to the originals. Most distilleries had promised to cooperate by then, but they were less than enthusiastic when it came to taking a subscription. In total, we only had ten distilleries, hardly 9% of the total. Duncan and Mark were rightly worried about the marketing that was mainly done via the Internet. Our joint optimism and fascination for the product did not leave much room for scepticism and we decided together to put more money into the promotion.

After the meeting was over, Duncan gave me a package and a note. On the note, which bore the coat of arms of Wallace Milroy, it said:

Dear Duncan,

Please give this to Hans
when he next arrives at your house.
Looking forward to seeing you soon.

Aye,
Wallace

The package contained a copy of the 7th edition of *The Malt Whisky Almanac.* On the title page, Wallace had written a personal message for me:

To Hans Offringa
Met vriendelijke groet
Jan. 1999

Please keep tasting all the wonderful malts from
Scotland (in moderation) especially at Craigellachie
Hotel – good friends, good food, what more does one
require. Here is volume II, to complete it again.

Best,
Wallace

"I phoned Wallace in November 1998, the day after you finished his almanac, to tell him this story." Duncan chuckled. "I knew he would send a new one. That's why I wrote Volume I in yours."

I could tell by the date that Wallace had reacted almost immediately to the phone call.

"I would like to meet him at some point," I said, and happily stared at the inscription in the book.

"He'll be here during the Speyside Festival. I will arrange something."

I did not stay in the hotel that night, but I drove to Elgin with Mark Lawson to spend the night with him and his wife Rosemarie, because the next morning I had to be in Elgin to pick up my kilt. A few months before, Bill Ross had told me it was time to purchase a Highland Dress with his tartan. He had after all accepted me into his clan. In earlier days, clan members were not necessarily related by blood or marriage. A clan chief could accept into the clan anyone he thought necessary. After joining, the person concerned was given protection in exchange for pledging his service to the clan.

Advised by Mark, I had gone to a specialised shop in Elgin to have my measurements taken and the kilt had been made to size. I had also selected the accompanying garments.

Now was the big moment. After breakfast, we went to McCall's. The fitting proved quite a ritual, but when I was finally fully dressed and standing in front of the mirror, a feeling of pride came over me. Proud of the fact that I had been accepted into the Clan Ross and was allowed to dress accordingly. I could hardly wait to get to St Fillans and arrived late that same afternoon. I immediately went upstairs to dress and 15 minutes later I appeared in the cosy living room of Earngrove Cottage. Bill was touched, Ulla enchanted and it meant more to me than I had expected. Before I owned a kilt, I used to rent one whenever I had to go to a whisky festival or present a tasting session. But from now on, I could wear my own kilt and tartan. I had chosen the modern hunting variant, which comes in a fresh green colour. The standard Ross tartan is red with dark blue. Most clans have different types of tartans, a dress one, a hunting one, etc. From that day on, the kilt travelled with me on my journeys between Scotland and the Netherlands, because I never knew when the opportunity to wear it would arise.

Back in the Netherlands, I dedicated myself once again to producing the whisky label encyclopaedia. The number of subscribers slowly increased. At the end of April we had 80 subscribers. We needed to have 300 at the end of 2000 to break even. The Speyside Festival was about to begin, which offered a fine opportunity to get some new converts to subscribe to our opus magnum. On 5 May, I left for The Craig, the night before the festivities started, which were to last until 8 May. Duncan Elphick had let me know that Wallace Milroy was to host a whisky dinner and wanted to meet me that afternoon before it started. I could hardly sleep that night. I kept thinking of 1994 when I had found the almanac on Guernsey and had decided to drink all these malts, unaware that I would meet the author in person, six years later.

The next morning crept by excruciatingly slowly. I was in the library working on a new novel, but I couldn't concentrate. My thoughts kept going to The Big Moment. Finally, it was two o'clock in the afternoon. I heard Duncan's voice coming from the corridor and footsteps approaching. The door swung open and two men entered, "Meet Wallace Milroy, Hans."

Wallace approached me with an outstretched hand. He was followed by Carol who entered with three glasses of whisky for us to toast on our getting acquainted.

"Slainte math. May I see the book?"

I took out my bible and gave it to the author who slowly turned the pages, smiling every now and again about a certain comment. He grabbed a pen and wrote on the title page:

Full marks upon completion.
You must have wonderful memories.
Best regards,
Wallace
Craigellachie 6 May 2000

After this we walked outside and Duncan took a picture of us in front of the hotel, in the sun. We spent the rest of that memorable afternoon together, talking, walking, drinking beer and whisky at a speed that was really too high for me. Wallace was like a full cask spilling over with stories and a very entertaining conversation partner. That evening he asked if I wanted to sit next to him during the whisky dinner. When all the guests were seated, Wallace stood up and said, "Please meet my assistant from Holland," and he nodded to the left. I was happy as can be.

Dinner was a tough job, especially after our intake of booze that afternoon. Each course, seven in total, was amply accompanied by a single malt that matched the tasting features of the different dishes. Wallace whispered to me, "Drown the whisky; otherwise you won't make it till the end of the evening."

His warning came a bit too late. I was stinking drunk by the time we started on dessert – Iced Raspberry with a 30-year-old Macallan – and the next morning, I did not remember how I had ended up in my room.

"You don't want to know, but you were not the only one," said Duncan at breakfast the next morning.

That meeting with Wallace marked the beginning of a friendship that has lasted till this day. Whenever we have a chance, we meet. Sometimes in London, where he and his brother run a liquor store in Soho, sometimes in Scotland and usually in The Craig.

The rest of 2000 was marked by my commuting. I alternated between the Netherlands and Scotland every few weeks and it seemed as if I had reached my goal of living in both countries. Whenever I visited a distiller or had a special meeting with someone, I asked him or her to write a comment in my little bible. I taped the picture of Wallace and me on page 13, and, suitably proud, I told anybody who wanted to hear it the story behind the almanac.

Craigellachie
Saturday, 3 May 2003, 11:00 pm

During dinner, Mr Bowmore regularly looks at the purple book next to my plate. At some point, he can no longer hide his curiosity and he asks me what it is.

While I hand him the book, I tell the story from 1994 until 2000 in a nutshell.

"You really drank them all? Even Kinclaith?"

I nod discreetly and immediately rise high in his opinion. Even the shelves of the Quaich bar no longer hold Kinclaith. Worldwide, there are maybe a few bottles left, owned by wealthy collectors. In 1997, I, still relatively ignorant, had bought a miniature at the Gordon & MacPhail whisky shop in Elgin to complete the K on the list in my almanac (I had already tried Knockando and Knockdhu in 1989 and 1994 respectively). Back in the Netherlands, I had drunk the miniature together with Rudolf and I had written in my little bible: '19/5/1997. Drank it at home. Fragrant and fruity. Slightly sweet. Bears repeating.'

My Norwegian friend is clearly impressed and congratulates me. He has not managed yet to add this extremely rare single malt to his collection. His wife says that it is time to go upstairs. There is a bus waiting to take us to The Macallan, a little ways further, on the opposite side of the Spey.

We are welcomed by the hosts Margaret Gray and Morag Ralph who explain to us what we are going to do. First we will take a walk to the graveyard on the grounds behind the warehouses. In the dark, by the light of a sin-

gle flashlight we, a group of twenty slightly intimidated whisky lovers, follow Margaret. The other group is with Morag. Suddenly we hear a blood-curling scream and we see a ghostly figure running for cover in the trees. A bit further a dark silhouette is being knocked down and stuck with a knife by two vandals who quickly flee in the direction of the stillhouse. It is done so realistically that we all grow quiet and a little nervous. When we arrive at the graveyard, Margaret asks us to enter, but no one moves, even less so when we see the ghost jump up from behind a tombstone and run to the small chapel.

Smiling secretly, Margaret indicates a wooden door, opens it and whispers that we all have to go inside and follow the long corridor. Timidly, we follow her orders. The corridor has a couple of corners leading left and right. We inch along, until we reach another door, which opens automatically. We enter a dusky, circular room and can see the contours of over 100 tasting glasses on a half-round table. Once we are all inside, Margaret asks us to be absolutely quiet. We all watch the entrance quite intently. All the lights go out, the door creaks and a minute later we are all in a brightly lit room. In front of us is the ghost of the graveyard; he yanks off his hideous head and a face appears from under the mask that belongs to Bob Dalgarno, the master noser and blender of Macallan. Everybody applauds, more than a bit relieved.

Bob presents a fine collection of Macallans of different ages and explains how the distillery takes extreme care to ensure the consistency of the taste. The highlight of the tasting is a Macallan from 1945. It has a taste that is slightly too woody and peaty for me, but still a welcome addition to my tasting notes. During the tasting, the other 'ghosts' arrive. It turns out they are all Macallan employees.

At two in the morning our bus drives us back to the hotel. The Speyside Festival has come to an end. Tomorrow we will all go home. Before we go up the staircase in the hall, my Norwegian friend asks me if he can become a member of the 'Friends of Craigellachie Malt Whisky Club.'

I smile and say, "We've got one space left."

Springbank 21-year-old
2001-2002

In 2001, travelling between Scotland and the Netherlands turned into a natural routine for me. To minimise the amount of luggage I had to carry from one place to the other, I had a limited wardrobe both in St Fillans and in Craigellachie. On my flights, I usually made do with carry-on luggage, including my trusted Apple Mac and a camera. On the Scottish side of the North Sea, I concentrated mainly on marketing the encyclopaedia. In the process, I got to know the less accommodating side of the whisky industry for which I had previously had so much respect. Whereas the whisky drinker appreciates variation, the distillery does not. They found the inclusion of their own distillery and their labels in the book a good idea, but to buy a copy that included the competitors' labels and to put that book in the visitor's centre went too far. This was a severe setback for us, because the group of over 1 million visitors per year was the perfect target group for us, one that, so far, we had exclusively tried to track by means of the Internet.

The encyclopaedia was a beautiful publication, but also one that needed to be sold. There were only a few people who had subscribed through the website, the rest of them had been approached personally by Mark, Duncan or me. At the end of 2000, we had sold about 100 copies and we needed to have 300. John LaDell had lost heart and did not want to write anymore. Mark offered to take over his share and John grabbed the opportunity with both hands. Duncan wanted to give it one more try and invited Jim Murray to The Craig to ask if he wanted to do some pioneering work. I flew to Scotland for this meeting. I had met Jim in 1998 and had spent some time with him. Even then, he was regarded the *enfant terrible* among whisky authors and I was not sure if we could get him to work with us. By 2001, he had already published a great many books and had managed to make as many friends as enemies in the whisky world. His participation would no doubt be controversial.

Jim was brief and to the point. Nice publication but not interested. It would distract him from his own books too much. I should have known. I had heard before that he didn't see the point of translating his books either. It would only harm the sales of the original English ones, which would have an effect on his royalties. While we were talking in the library, he picked up the excellent publication of Charlie MacLean's *Malt Whisky* between thumb and index finger, and with a dirty look, he dropped it behind the sofa. I knew he hated Charles, but I didn't think it was funny. The world of whisky authors is a fairly small one, with plenty of room for everybody, and you don't treat your colleagues like that. I met Charles for the first time in 2003, and I found him to be a real gentleman. You couldn't say the same of Jim. The fact remains however, that he is one of the greatest whisky authors of his time and an incredible expert at that.

To ease the pain, Jim gave me a signed copy of *The Art of Whisky*, a nicely produced book that includes pictures of whisky posters from the past.

Jim Murray's refusal resulted in Duncan Elphick

abandoning the project. Now it was my turn to take over someone's shares. From that moment on, Mark and I were the joint owners of a Scottish publishing house with only one product that was losing money. We kept it up until the end of 2001. With 125 subscribers our only option was to kill the project. We settled all bills and liquidated the company. The encyclopaedia had cost us some tens of thousands of pounds. Mark was left with a fascination for publishing and not much later started Librario.com, a company that helped authors publish books directly. I was left with a collection of over 2,500 labels I might use for some project in the future. We licked our wounds and started thinking of other plans.

2001 was not my year anyway. I was too busy with my own publishing house in the Netherlands, and had too little time to write. The best parts of that year were my nosing and tasting sessions that increased rapidly in number. In the Netherlands, but also in Germany, Belgium and Scotland. At the end of the year, I took stock of my life, sold my publishing house to a larger one, concentrated fully on writing, booked a flight to Edinburgh where Bill picked me up from the airport, and locked myself up in St Fillans to work on the plot of my new novel, with half of the story taking place in Scotland and the other half in the Netherlands.

Relieved of the stress that comes with running a company, my creativity bloomed and the story soon took shape. With May 2002 came another Speyside Festival and I decided to complete the first version of the manuscript in the library of the Craigellachie Hotel.

Duncan was happy to see me after all this time, because I had not been to Craigellachie since the collapse of the encyclopaedia. One of the whisky authors I had never met, but who had kept me engaged with his *World Guide to Whisky* since 1987, was Michael Jackson. Duncan knew that I wanted to meet him of course, and it was no coincidence that Michael and I met in the library of The Craig. This room was taking on mythical proportions for me, due to all the things that had happened to me there. It was very special to meet the man whose books I had been using for the past seventeen years as a source of information. In front of him was the 4th edition of the *Companion.*

"I understood from Duncan that you write and publish."

I nodded and we were soon engaged in a conversation and in the process he invited me to a whisky and beer tasting in the drawing room. Just before we started, he gave me a copy of the 4th edition and said it had a message for me. I opened the book and read:

To Hans,
I hope you will translate and publish the 5th edition.
Proost!
Michael Jackson
Craigellachie, Scotland, 4 May 2002

During the beer & whisky tasting, I met Hideo Yamaoka, Michael's Japanese translator and publisher and a member of the famous Friends club. After the tasting, together with Michael and Martine Nouet, we finished an entire bottle of Springbank 21-year-old, one of the finest single malts in Scotland.

Thanks to Duncan Elphick I had not only been able to try all the different Scotch single malts, but I had also met the very top of the world of whisky authors. After the Festival, I stayed on at The Craig for another week to finish the manuscript and I returned to the Netherlands content and with only one dream left: to meet Charlie MacLean. I did not know at the time that my tall, grey-haired friend was already undertaking actions to arrange this.

Craigellachie
Friday, 2 May 2003, 10:30 am

I am standing in the hall with my suitcase, talking to Carol while her assistant is getting the bill. One by one, the guests walk down the beautiful wooden staircase, shaking hands and saying goodbye. Each of them off to a different destination, somewhere in the world. The Craigellachie Hotel – a timeless presence in an ever-changing world. The majority of the guests I will see again next year, but each year there are new surprises and meetings to be enjoyed. After I have settled the bill, I kiss Carol goodbye and give Duncan a bear hug.

"See you soon," he says and walks outside with me to send me off. When I turn onto the A95 to Aberlour, I see a grey-haired, tall man walking to the bungalow behind the hotel. Duncan is going to get his spaniels to go for a walk and, no doubt, he is thinking about who the next person will be who has managed to find the road to Craigellachie.

Half an hour later, I take the A9 to Perth and put my foot right down; three hours later, I park the car behind Earngrove Cottage. Bill opens the back door and walks to the car to get my suitcase.

"I think I'm going to write a book about whisky," I tell him. He puts an arm around me and replies,

"First finish your second novel, son, first finish the novel."

Oban
2002-2003

Back in my mother country, I took the manuscript of my novel to my editor. Four weeks later, I got it back with a note saying, "Interesting story, but sometimes it reads like a travel guide to Scotland." In practice this resulted in many days of taking out parts, rewriting, adapting, and checking the consistency of the entire book. She has almost always been right so far, and she was right this time. I took out the extreme travel passages and saved them in a separate document, thinking they might come in handy later. Two versions and five months later, I got the go-ahead for my publication. My second novel became a reality.

To celebrate, I left for my 'father country' and christened the book together with Bill and Ulla, killing a bottle of Oban in the process. They had to laugh about the anecdote of my editor and the travel guide, and even though they did not read Dutch, they still got some of the inside jokes in the book. I had put in some of the names and houses of a few villagers in St Fillans, including theirs, as well as some of Ulla's idiosyncrasies.

I sat staring at the flames of the open fire, a contented man, and felt reborn in my Scottish parental home. The year 2002 was drawing to a close and I wondered what I would be doing in the year to come.

"When do you start with the whisky book?"

"Early next year, Bill."

"You kept some of the stuff your editor told you to take out of this one?"

"I did."

"Use it for the new book and make it a road novel."

"I might do that."

"And then call it *The Road to Craigellachie*!"

"Thanks Bill, I like that title."

After Hogmanay, I left St Fillans, having been warmed and nourished, and turned once again to writing.

When Duncan called me in the Netherlands mid-April 2003 to announce that he had set up a meeting with Charlie MacLean for the upcoming Speyside Festival, I had completed a fair part of *The Road to Craigellachie*.

"When do you expect me, Duncan?"

"Thursday 1 May, Hans!"

"I'll be there, Duncan!"

"You'd better!"

I put down the phone, walked to my laptop, and booked a ticket.

As Robert Burns once wrote, 'Freedom an' Whisky gang thegither...'

Earngrove Cottage, where I met Bill.

Epilogue 2011

Since The Road was first published in 2004, various things have happened. The Vikings sold the Craigellachie Hotel, which is now run by a different manager. It retains an iconic status as a whisky hotel with its tremendous Quaich Bar.

Duncan Elphick left the hotel but not the eponymous village. He bought ownership in the Highlander Inn on the opposite side of the street and created a cosy country hotel, perfectly complementing the opportunities to stay in Craigellachie.

Lesley Ann Parker moved from Buckie to Craigellachie and started an art gallery next to her design studio. She became a dear friend and promotes my books whenever she can. She is also heavily involved in the Moray Chamber of Commerce, further developing the economy in the area with outstanding ideas.

I still see Carol Brown, who has been working at The Macallan for several years. It is always a pleasure to meet her, Morag and Margaret, especially at Macallan.

Joe Brandie is running the Fiddichside Inn on his own, surprising and pleasing the village and its visitors by keeping it open after the sad loss of his wife, Dorothy.

I finally made it to Jack Daniel's where I became a Tennessee Squire. I have now visited Lynchburg and its delightful residents on numerous occasions.

Martine Nouet contributed to my book *A Taste of Whisky* and we keep in touch on a regular basis. I have had the pleasure of working frequently with Charles

MacLean, among other things contributing chapters to his *Whisky* (Eyewitness Companions) and *World Whisky*. Dave Broom reviewed the manuscript of my *Whisky & Jazz* and kindly wrote the foreword.

And indeed, I did translate into Dutch Michael Jackson's 5th edition of the *Malt Whisky Companion* as well as his magnum opus *Whisky – The Definitive World Guide*. In the course of time we became close friends and remained so until his sudden death on 30 August 2007.

The last time I saw my beloved Scottish faither, William Ross, was on his 80th birthday in May 2009. Only months later he died unexpectedly and I miss him deeply.

People around the world still send me emails asking for tips, which I happily supply. The responses I get later are often very amusing to read. The more whisky lovers, the better.

As of today I have written and translated a considerable series of whisky books. Some of them are not only published in Dutch and English but also in French. Thanks to my fellow whisky writers, to my many readers in various countries and to the whisky industry at large I can continue to write and feel encouraged by them in exploring new insights into the drink of drinks.

Thank you all!

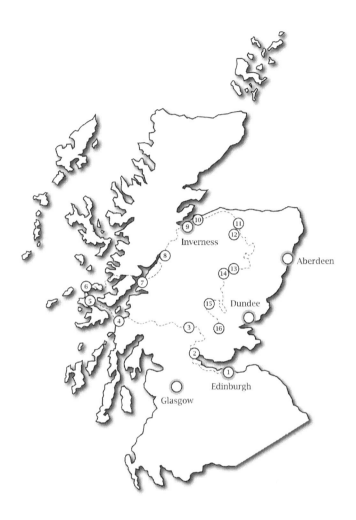

1 Edinburgh
2 Stirling Castle
3 St Fillans
4 Oban
5 Tobermory (Mull)
6 Kilchoan
7 Fort William
8 Loch Ness

9 Inverness
10 Culloden
11 Craigellachie
12 Glenfarclas
13 Balmoral/Lochnagar
14 Braemar
15 Pitlochry
16 Perth

Trip 1
Starting point Edinburgh

Day 1

Edinburgh is a good place to start, and it can easily be reached by plane since several airlines offer a number of flights to Edinburgh each day. A ferry can also be taken from the Netherlands, but this will mean a full day of travelling.

Day 2

There are many hotels and B&Bs in Edinburgh. A nice stretch for a walk is the Royal Mile from Holyrood Palace to Edinburgh Castle. The Scotch Whisky Experience is located near the castle. A visit to this museum is amusing, interesting and educational. You can take a tour seated in a motorised (empty) whisky cask, which takes you past three ages of whisky history.

Day 3

From Edinburgh, take the M9 north. After about 30 minutes, you will get to Stirling Castle, on the right. In the distance you will see the Wallace Memorial, where Braveheart's sword is displayed. After you have visited both sites, you will have enough time to drive on to Crieff and visit the Glenturret distillery. Next, follow the A85 west, in the direction of Crianlarich. Fifteen minutes from Crieff there is a choice of hotels or B&Bs in St Fillans.

Day 4

After spending the night in St Fillans, turn west taking
the A85. There is a fine whisky shop in Tyndrum, on the
right side of the road. Stay on the A85 and you will get
to Oban, a harbour town, named after a wonderful west-
highland malt with a hint of sea wind (or maybe it was
the other way round).

Day 5

Oban is a good starting point for exploring the Isle of
Mull. Take the car ferry run by Caledonian McBrayne
(www.calmac.co.uk), the company that has the monopoly
on ferry transport in this part of Scotland, and it will
take you to Tobermory, a beautiful little harbour town
with coloured houses and a distillery by the same name,
which also produces a single malt whisky under the
name of Ledaig.

Day 6

Take the early morning ferry from Tobermory to Kilchoan on the Ardnamurchan peninsula. It is a very small
ferry that can only take two to three cars at a time. On
the other side, take the B8007 east. This is a breathtakingly beautiful by-road that will take you to the A861.
Take the A861 east, and then take the ferry to Corran
at Ardgour. Then take the A82 north and you will reach
Fort William at the end of the day, just in time to visit the
Ben Nevis distillery.

Day 7

Follow the A82 north until you reach Fort Augustus, located on the southwest point of Loch Ness. From there, follow the west coast of the famous loch. Stop at Urquhart Castle, or rather the ruins of the castle, from where you can walk straight to the loch. This is a great place for monster spotting. The Nessie shop in near Drumnadrochit sells Loch Ness water that is 10,000 years old, indispensable for a special dram! Continue north and spend the night in Inverness, the capital of the Highlands.

Day 8

A little east of Inverness, on the A96, you will find Culloden Battlefield, where Scottish victims of the last British civil war are buried. Several clans have their own stone. At the visitor's centre, drink a dram for the repose of the deceased. Stay on the A96 in eastern direction until you reach Elgin. Visit the impressive ruins of the cathedral. Then turn south using the A941. You will pass a fair number of distilleries, among which Glen Rothes, Longmorn and Glen Grant. Stop at Craigellachie to spend the night.

Day 9

If you discovered the Quaich Bar in Craigellachie last night and if you studied their vast collection of single malts, you probably need a day's rest. The surroundings of the village are quite scenic. The Speyside Way (a walking path) passes in front of the hotel and the Speyside Cooperage, two miles in the direction of Dufftown, is also worth a visit. In the evening, go have a pint at the Fiddichside Inn, the smallest pub of Scotland.

Day 10

You are in the heart of the Speyside and you probably want to explore a few more distilleries. From Craigella- chie, it is only five minutes to Macallan, five minutes to Aberlour, five minutes to Glenfiddich, twenty minutes to Glenfarclas, Cardhu and a handful of less well-known distilleries. Strathisla is thirty minutes away, as is Glen- livet. Be sure to have a pint or a dram at the Highlander Inn, home to not only an impressive collection of sin- gle malts, but also of the "Crac" – Craigallechie Real Ale Club.

Day 11

For the sake of variation, you can also visit a number of castles, Ballindalloch for instance, which is diagonally opposite Glenfarclas. Or Fyvie Castle which is a bit fur- ther to the east and which can be combined with a visit to the Glendronach distillery. You can spend the night near here, if you like.

Day 12

From Craigellachie, take the A941 south, another beau- tiful road that will take you through the Cabrach. At Rhynie, turn right onto the A97 and follow it until you reach the A93. Then turn right and follow the River Dee. After a short while you will reach Balmoral Castle, the Scottish home of the British royal family. Do not forget to visit Royal Lochnagar to drink a royal dram. Then fol- low the A93 through Braemar and turn right at the Bridge of Calley to Pitlochry (A924) and spend the night in the Moulin Hotel for instance.

Day 13

Start your day by visiting The Edradour, the smallest commercial distillery of Scotland. Then go south taking the A9 to Perth where the A9 becomes the M90, and this will take you back to Edinburgh in an hour.

Day 14

In Leith, the old harbour of Edinburgh, you will find the headquarters of the Scotch Malt Whisky Society (www. smws.com). This society buys casks straight from the distilleries and bottles the whisky unfiltered and undiluted at set times. The labels have two numbers on them, one for the distillery, and one for the cask, and two years, one for distillation and one for bottling. This place is worth a visit before you return home.

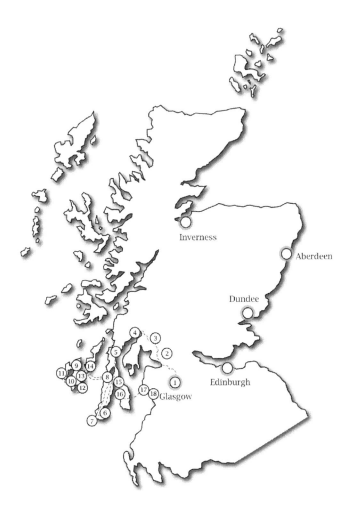

1 Glasgow
2 Gartocharn
3 Tarbet
4 Inverary
5 Lochgilphead
6 Campbeltown
7 Mull of Kintyre
8 Kennacraig
9 Port Askaig

10 Bowmore
11 Loch Gorm
12 Lagavulin
13 Caol Ila
14 Craighouse
15 Claonaig
16 Lochranza
17 Ardrossan
18 Stevenston

Trip 2
Starting point Glasgow

Day 1

Glasgow is also a good starting point for a holiday in Scotland. It can easily be reached by plane. Upon your arrival, visit the Charles Rennie Macintosh House or the famous Burrell Museum. The University is also well worth a visit. Much of Scotch whisky is bottled in Glasgow.

Day 2

Leave Glasgow in northwesterly direction by way of the A82. Turn right at Balloch, go to Gartocharn and stop for a cup of coffee at the Hungry Monk. Then turn back and take the A82 north. You will reach Loch Lomond, for which Lomond distillery is named. They produce both a grain and a malt whisky for their own Inchmurrin malt, as well as for blends, including Old Rhosdhu. Drive on and turn left at Tarbet, taking the A83 and drive to Inveraray to spend the night.

Day 3

Inveraray offers various sights: the castle, the prison and the Loch Fyne whisky shop. The owner of the castle is the Duke of Argyll, head of Clan Campbell. There is also a blended whisky called Clan Campbell, but there is something unsettling about the name. A couple of ages ago, after a party, the Campbells slaughtered the MacDonalds in Glen Coe, the Valley of Weeping. The two clans never really got on after that.

Day 4

Be prepared for a long drive south. The A83 will take you all the way to Campbeltown, the smallest whisky region in Scotland. Along the way, you will go through Lochgilphead, which plays an important part in Iain Banks' hilarious novel *The Crow Road*. Campbeltown is home to the Springbank, Glengyle and Glen Scotia distilleries. In the early 19th century there were over 30 distilleries there.

Day 5

Southwest of Campbeltown is the Mull of Kintyre, which has been so gracefully serenaded by Paul McCartney. Take an early stroll along the beach and then return to Campbeltown and drive to Claonaig by way of the B824. Then take the B8001 to cross to Kennacraig and take the ferry to the isle of Islay. Be prepared for a fine crossing that takes nearly two-and-a-half hours. Whether you arrive in Port Askaig or Port Ellen you will find charming B&Bs nearby.

Day 6

Take the A846 to Bridgend and then on to Bowmore on Loch Indaal. Visit the Bowmore distillery with its famous warehouses below sea level. At the distillery, try to get a taste of the 17-year-old version of this great Islay malt: it's a must! On the other side is Bruichladdich, where the lightest malt of the island is produced. Meet Jim McEwan, the distillery manager, and a monument in the whisky industry.

Day 7

Spend the day exploring another part of the island. First head to Kilchoman Distillery (turn off the A847 between Bridgend and Bruichladdich) for a tour of a real working farm distillery. Then try out the by-roads that take you around nearby Loch Gorm and finish with a hike around Ardnave Point north of the Nature Reserve.

Day 8

From Bowmore, drive south to Port Ellen. This used to be a distillery but is now the maltings for the other distilleries on the island. A little west of the harbour town, you will find three heavies: Laphroaig, Lagavulin and Ardbeg. Visiting them all in one day is doable, but only for diehards. Be sure to carefully check tour times.

Day 9

Drive to Port Askaig, turn left and a meandering road will lead you to Bunnahabhain, one of the two distilleries that are still in operation on the east side of the island. South of port Askaig, you will find number two: Caol Ila, which offers a terrific view of the Paps of Jura from the stillroom.

Day 10

From Port Askaig, make the crossing to Jura to taste The Isle of Jura in Craighouse. There are palm trees here, due to the warm Gulf Stream that hugs the shores of the island. If you are a nature-lover and a deer-lover (there are more deer on this Hebrides isle than there are people) spend the night in the only hotel on Jura.

Kildalton Cross, Islay

Barnhill House, where George Orwell wrote his science fiction novel *1984*, is a several mile hike past the end of the main paved road.

Day 11

To return to the Argyll peninsula you will have to travel by way of Islay because there is no direct route to the mainland. From Islay, you can sail back to Kennacraig and once again, use the B8001 to get to Claonaig, where you can take the ferry to Arran. This will lead you to Lochranza, where you can spend the night.

Day 12

You cannot avoid tasting an Arran single malt here. Slainte! (Gaelic for 'cheers'). The distillery produces a malt whisky called Isle of Arran and a blend named Lochranza. The town is a pretty one, and offers many sightseeing opportunities.

Day 13

Spending an extra day on the Isle of Arran is worth it. The island is sometimes called 'little Scotland'. There are many prehistoric sights, among which the Auchagallon Stone Circle, a rudimentary version of Stonehenge.

Day 14

Take the ferry from Brodick to Ardrossan, and then take the A78 south. At Stevenston, the A738 and A737 will take you back to the airport of Glasgow.

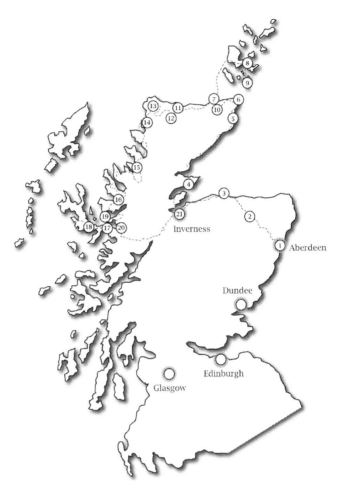

1 Aberdeen
2 Huntly
3 Elgin
4 Tain
5 Wick
6 John o'Groats
7 Scrabster
8 Kirkwall
9 South Ronaldsay
10 Thurso
11 Coldbackie
12 Tongue
13 Cape Wrath
14 Laxford Bridge
15 Ullapool
16 Loch Torridon
17 Kyle of Lochalsh
18 Sconser
19 Plockton
20 Eilean Donan
21 Inverness

Trip 3
Starting point Aberdeen

Day 1

Aberdeen, the oil city of Scotland, is a good start for the third trip, which will take you to the far north and north-west of Scotland. For those who love driving. The A96 will take you straight to Inverness. Huntly (ruins of a castle), Keith (Strathisla Distillery) and Elgin (cathedral and over 10 distilleries in walking distance) are great places to stop along the way. Inverness has a variety of B&Bs and hotels.

Day 2

Take the A9 north. The landscape slowly gets wilder and less populated. The people of Tain and Glenmorangie peacefully distil whisky. The name of this well-known malt whisky does indeed mean 'valley of tranquility'. You will pass the twins Brora/Clynelish and close to Wick you will find Old Pulteney. Take the A99 and stop at John O'Groats to spend the night.

Day 3

You are in the hometown of Scotland's Last House. You are close to the Stacks of Duncansby, a dark version of the ragged cliffs of the Isle of Wight, on the other side of Great Britain. Drive on in westerly direction until you reach Scrabster. Take the ferry to Orkney and you will land in Stromness.

Day 4

It's time to visit a distillery: Highland Park, currently the most northerly distillery of Scotland, located in Kirkwall, the capital of the Orkney isles.

Day 5

The Orkneys have been inhabited since pre-historic times. In 1840, a hamlet dating back over 5,000 years was discovered near Skara Brae on Mainland, the main isle. A visit here is worthwhile.

Day 6

In Kirkwall, you will find St Magnus Cathedral, which was built by the Vikings in the 11th century and which is built of red bricks. This is a good opportunity to explore this unique building. Legend has it that whisky was put in the pulpit to hide it from the English customs officials.

Day 7

The Standing Stones of Stennes, also on Mainland, stem from the same period as Skara Brae. Some of them rise over six meters above ground, and they have suffered from the wind and erosion, but are still standing. There are hardly any trees on Orkney. A bit further, you can see the Ring of Brodgar, which, according to many, is the most beautiful Stone Circle on the British Isles. Maeze Howe, also close to Stennes, is a crypt adorned with runes that were written by the Vikings some thousands of years ago. Graffiti *avant la lettre*!

Day 8

On South Ronaldsay, the southern-most isle of the Orkneys, you will find the Tomb of the Eagles on the land of
an old farmer. By all means, have a stiff dram before you
crawl into the tomb. You will find a row of skulls from
3000 BC. On the farmer's land, remains from a house
built in the Iron Age have been laid bare.

Day 9

After all this history, the time has come to visit the other
distillery on the Orkneys: Scapa, two thirds of a mile further south than Highland Park, on the Scapa Flow, which
is where the German marine sank its fleet at the end of
World War I, after hearing the terms of the Treaty of Ver-
sailles. Take the afternoon ferry back to the mainland of
Scotland. You can spend the night in Thurso.

Day 10

Leave Thurso in westerly direction and stay on the A836.
You will pass the beach of Coldbackie, one of the most
beautiful and cleanest beaches of Western Europe, mainly because of the lack of mass tourism. Take the A838 at
Tongue and drive north, around Loch Eriboll and find a
B&B in Durness before Cape Wrath. There are no distilleries in this remote part of Scotland, but the scenery is a
breathtaking accompaniment to a dram. Sleep well.

Kilt Rock, Isle of Skye

Day 11

Get up early for a magnificent drive through a breathtaking landscape. Follow the A838 until Laxford Bridge and turn right and take the A894, which will turn into the A837. At Ledmore Junction, turn right onto the A835. You will pass Ullapool. After Braemore, turn right taking the A832 and follow it until Kinlochewe. Turn right again, to take the A896. The Torridon Hotel is impressive, yet costly.

Day 12

Follow the A896 west and turn right at New Kelso to go to Kyle of Lochalsh. Cross the Skye Bridge and follow the A87 until you have passed Sconser. Then turn left to take the A863 and not much after, you will see Talisker, the only distillery on the Isle of Skye. After your visit to the distillery, follow the road in the opposite direction to leave Skye by the same bridge. Drive to Plockton, one of the most picturesque villages on the west coast, with palm trees and hydrangea along the shore.

Day 13

From Plockton back to Aberdeen. Follow the A87 for the first part of the trip; this beautiful road will take you past Eilean Donan, the most photographed castle of Scotland. Turn left at the crossing, to go north, and take the A887, which will become the A82 and will take you past the shores of Loch Ness to Inverness. Then take the A96 east. After about four hours of driving you will be back in Aberdeen. Have a good flight home.

Recommended Reading

Barnard, Alfred. *The Whisky Distilleries of the United Kingdom*. Originally published by Harpers in 1887. Facsimile republication by Kwisinski and Sagemann, 2000. ISBN 3934005845.

Broom, Dave. *The World Atlas of Whisky*. Mitchell Beazley 2010. ISBN 9781845335410.

Buxton, Ian. *101 Whiskies to Try Before You Die*. Hachette Scotland 2010. ISBN 9780755360833.

Gils, Marcel van, and Hans Offringa. *The Legend of Laphroaig*. Still Publishing 2007. ISBN 9789089100276.

Hanley, Cliff. *History of Scotland*. Lomond Books, 1994. ISBN 09477820176.

Hills, Phillip. *Appreciating Whisky*. HarperCollins Publishers, 2000. ISBN 0004724496.

Jackson, Michael. *The Malt Whisky Companion*. 5th edition. Dorling Kindersley, 2004. ISBN 1405302348.

Jackson, Michael. *WHISKY – The Definitive Guide*. Dorling Kindersley Ltd, 2005. ISBN 0751344346.

MacLean, Charles. *Scotch, a liquid history*. Cassell Illustrated, 2004. ISBN 1844034011.

MacLean, Charles et al. *Eyewitness Companions Whisky.*
Dorling Kindersley, 2010. ISBN 9781405328142.

Milroy, Wallace and Neil Wilson. *Whisky in Your Pocket –*
based on The Original Malt Whisky Almanac.
Waverley Books 2010. ISBN 9781849340236.

Murray, Jim. *The Whisky Bible.* 8th edition
Dram Good Books 2010. ISBN 9780955472954.

Nouet, Martine. *Les Routes du Malt.* Hermé, 1999.
ISBN 2866653033.

Offringa, Hans. *A Taste of Whisky.* 2nd Edition.
Conceptual Continuity 2009. ISBN 9789089100078.

Paterson, Richard and Gavin D. Smith. *Goodness Nose*
The Passionate Revelations of a Scotch Whisky Master
Blender. Angels' Share 2008. ISBN 9781903238677.

Ronde, Ingvar. *Malt Whisky Yearbook 2011.*
MagdigMedia Ltd, 2010. ISBN 9780955260773.

Wishart, David. *Whisky Classified.* 2nd edition.
Pavilion Books, 2006. ISBN 1862057168.

Other publications by the author

Whisky books
Bourbon & Blues
Whisky & Jazz
A Taste of Whisky
The Legend of Laphroaig
Nightcaps
The Whisky Calendar
Whisky Almanak
Classic Malts Selection
Scotch Whisky – The Box:
  Malt Whisky
  Blended Whisky
  Taste of Scotland

Translations into Dutch
The Malt Whisky Companion (M. Jackson)
WHISKY – The Definitive World Guide (M. Jackson)
Whisky Classified (D. Wishart)
Collins Gem of Whisky (C. Shaw)
Whisky (Eyewitness Companions) (C. MacLean et al)
World Atlas of Whisky (D. Broom)

Whisky articles for
The Charleston Mercury
The Malt Advocate
Whisky etc.
Whisky Magazine
Whisky Passion

Novels
The House
Departure
The Composed Grandchild

Historical books
Raising the Kursk
Zwolle, a culinary delight
Bad luck, I'm from Zwolle
St. Bonifatius Park
Champagne de Luxe:
    The Tradition
    The Taste
Golf - The Box:
    How and Why
    Who, Where and When

Illustrated books (with Agnita Ratelband)
The Directors Book
Cowbook
Hobbyhorses